The Reluctant Tarot Reader

Adventures in the Gypsy Trade

Raven Mardirosian

Jai Ma.

CONTENTS

BEGINNINGS:
THE FOOL, THE COYOTE, THE REAL ME

"What do you do?" is usually the first question upon meeting someone.

Not — "Who are you?" or "Where do you come from?" *What* defines *who*.

Why?

Eckhart Tolle is mumbling something about consciousness being unconscious from his audiobook, *A New Earth: Awakening to Your Life's Purpose* but I'm too busy screaming, "Goddamn it! The speed limit is 50, not 30!" I'm late for my 12-6 shift at Pyramid Wellness and clients will be patiently waiting on the couch as I rush in. Everyone is on the road because it is back to school time. *Everyone* meaning six cars on the two lane stretch of Rt. 103 to Rutland.

Six is five too many.

More like water, less like rock. More like wah . . . god-damn it!

It's time to cover myself in white light and pray to the goddess / god / angels / guides / teachers and all interested parties but I can't get past this *total asshole* who insists on braking at every inopportune moment. The snooty Prius who plays the unfortunate middle man revs his engine and zooms past our mutual trouble. I'm left with the backside of a dented van holding Vermont plates, which generally grants my traveling mercies.

Not today. I'm a madwoman in my Subie at 11:52 a.m.

Expansion of consciousness. I wish. How about expansion of lanes?

Chill out, girl. Get it together. Everything's fine. I hate being late. Shit. Control freak. Perfectionist. Why can't I be more Zen? Okay, crack a joke immediately upon entrance. People will see that I'm in touch with my rage, yet can make light of it.

Sure. Try fooling a roomful of intuitives. As I confidently swoop in, my friend Bill smiles and asks, "How's it going, Raven?"

I blow out a breath, smile and shrug. "I'm here," I say.

My metaphysical crew. We're all lunatics with big love in our hearts. If only I could embrace my inner lunatic. I'm trying. Why can't I accept that I'm human? What is the crime in showing frustration? It doesn't make me a fraud. Divine Well-Being still exists . . . and maybe even chuckling somewhere. A crap drive doesn't negate me being an effective reader.

Hold on. Let me try that again.

An effective Tarot reader.

That sounds a little crazy. Kind of foolish. Maybe I should find a *real job.*

Trust me, I never wanted to be a Tarot reader.

During a street festival last summer, a man came up after noticing my sign and asked about a session. He seemed a little shocked that I charged well for my work.

"I thought readings were done for fun at parties," he said.

"Actually, this is how I make a living," I replied.

He turned and walked away.

It's humbling to know that I've gone from respected English teacher to a walking party favor. Maybe it's time to up my rates.

It also makes me miss the previous built-in "what do you do?" answer: teacher. Even better, New York City high school English teacher. Throw in *South Bronx* and respect went through the roof. *Artist* or *writer* gets the same admiring look.

But *Tarot reader?* Usually there's a confused glance mixed with a bit of fascination. Or they simply shrink away. I often say *intuitive* which adds to the confusion. I've never cared for the label *psychic*. Way too much stigma. *Healer?* No one really gets that one, either.

Tarot reader. It's not like I grew up dreaming of the day I'd own my first deck. How could I? My family was strictly evangelical Presbyterian. Born-again. Fundamentalist Christians to the core. Church as much as possible. No room for anything save a literal interpretation of the Bible. Tarot reading wasn't on the list of sanctified practices or viable career choices. I occasionally shook a Magic 8 ball but Tarot? No clue. Ouija boards freaked me out. I shoved everything mysterious into a New Age box full of witches, sorcerers and evil spirits to avoid at all cost, as my soul was at stake.

It's difficult to explain evangelical Christianity if you haven't experienced its power. God is an *all-consuming fire,* so count on being swallowed up or burned. Either way, the effects linger long past the intensity.

That old-school way of living — steady job, go to church, be married until you die —constantly dogged my natural bent towards independence. I called my 20s the "tyranny of the shoulds" (thank you, Karen Horney). The roaring portfolio '90s fit perfectly with the Protestant work ethic and crushing sense of responsibility emulated by my Depression-era parents. Work your life to the bone, give up every real dream and hope to have a little rest before you keel over. My parents focused on life in heaven. It was their biggest investment on this planet and they never let me forget it.

The human condition fascinates me, so early on I plunged into the world of books. I wrote constantly in a journal. Vet, missionary, English professor. Those were the paths for me.

Yet I'm a wanderer born under a Gemini sun, Aquarius moon and Scorpio rising. This was an astrological fact even when my Christian mind abhorred anything that smacked of soothsaying. Thank God/dess for the twelve houses of natal witness. I had little else when it came to my birth and subsequent adoption: a hastily scribbled paragraph of genealogy lay folded in my wallet for years. Gemini. The communicator. Freedom. The butterfly of the zodiac. In other words, the one who asks all of those annoying questions and slips away when you get on my nerves.

I'm extremely sensitive to moods, so excruciating headaches were the norm when I lived with my family. Of course, I turned to the Bible for answers but was left with a persistent guilt that dogged my every thought. I wouldn't learn the definition of *empath* until years later.

The irony was that I was never more afraid of failure and death than when I was a Christian. An austere Father God remained distressingly remote. I truly believed Jesus when he promised abundant life. However, that promise receded with each step out of the bounds of Christianity.

Everything terrified me.

I was a good girl and attended Christian school from 7th grade through college. Skirts and honor rolls. Banquets instead of proms. Gay kids doing their very best to be straight. I studiously avoided anywhere that held even a hint of hedonism. Christian bookstores were my refuge. Amy Grant was my girl crush. My tiny world was ruled by fear and doubt, though many viewed me as a confident leader. It only added to the confusion.

It was a long and convoluted path to the Tarot, but life has an uncanny way of sending teachers for this reluctant student. My schooling began with a couple of Catholic nuns in upstate New York who ran a retreat center. The church was long in my rearview by age 28. I desperately needed time away from a tumultuous relationship — most of the tumult being inside me — and go to what I knew best and missed most: Nature. Trees surrounded my Boerum Hill 'hood, but I grew tired of sharing them with thousands of strangers. I longed for the peace and stillness of the woods. No freakin' humans.

I didn't have any beef with Catholics. By that point in my evolution, prayers to Mary were cool and not a highway to hell. Still didn't take to the whole priest-as-ruler thing but the South Bronx nuns with whom I once worked were the most compassionately tough women on the planet. They had the undying thanks from the community and literally saved lives.

The retreat nuns were more than likely a couple but detecting subtle lesbianism on the Catholic level proved tricky. Protestant lesbians have different boundaries: less likely to live and work together unless it is in "reparative ministries". I viewed their bedrooms while touring the main house: one larger bed neatly made and the twin bed convincingly mussed. I've de-gayed enough rooms to know the deal. Though they invited me to dinner, I politely declined as my city walls were firmly up.

The following afternoon, I sat by a lovely pond about a stone's throw from the meditation room and mentally swirled around the wreck of my life. It was a perfectly beautiful day that couldn't penetrate my soul. My mood was quietly desperate, a regular condition of my 20s. The weekend faded as I removed myself from the ending — like when a gorgeous woman smiled at me, yet I couldn't muster up enough courage to approach. Her warmth only cast little icicles over my heart. Did I really believe that she wanted me? *Me?*

Nature, my comfort and solace could only touch the edges. God wasn't to be found and an anxious girlfriend awaited my decision. Stay— or go?

I was lost. Completely, totally lost. A perfectly good English degree lay at the bottom of my underwear drawer. I was young, attractive and thrived on the City's energy which conveniently matched the huge chip on my shoulder.

Lost and starting to worry that this condition would plague the remainder of what I hoped was a very short life. I was weary of New York, weary of love and lugging around this constant, ragged wound.

The nuns kept a respectful distance. As I staggered up — always trying to *be cool, be cool, be cool* — they approached and nonchalantly said hello. Gotta love nuns. They have perfected the art of detached concern. I tried my best to be courteous and prove that I was *fine* but they knew better. The gruffer one held out a palm-sized box.

"I thought you might like these," she said.

Circular playing cards? From Catholic nuns? If I was lost before, this merely added to the puzzle. It must have shown on my face.

"The Motherpeace Tarot. See what you think." She gently placed the deck in my hands.

Old Christian ghosts instantly materialized — but emotional devastation tends to blow open new doors. What did I have to lose?

The cards held the strangest images — women flying, dancing, swords on fire. I didn't have a clue what anything meant; didn't know the order, the story or how they worked. Plus, the fear of demonic influences quickly put a damper on my little party.

You can take the girl outta the church but try taking the church outta the girl.

I shuffled, then put them aside to write even more heart-twisting journal entries. I cried. I masturbated. The woods began withdrawing into themselves. The air was crisp and autumnal and I was alone.

After a long nap, I came back to the deck. The visuals captured my curiosity and soothed my soul in a way that the Bible hadn't. Since it came from nuns, Tarot couldn't be entirely evil. Could it? Either way, the cards helped to clear up the sad picture of my life with the beautiful scholar. It was time to move on.

I wish I could remember the first card I drew. Queen of Swords? Perhaps. A bit of a control freak. My notion of control then was a scorched earth policy: *freedom* meant leaving on vague, uncertain terms after lazily belittling the woman I loved. Everything was her fault.

Or maybe it was the Eight of Cups. Letting go — the constant, irritating mantra of my existence. When I was 22 and living on Cape Cod, my first love and I spent a weekend in the gay mecca of Provincetown. Our quickly fragmenting relationship was in direct contrast to the nervous excitement of my newborn lesbian "lifestyle".

We cuddled on the dunes. The sun was beginning to set, a blissful moment that some horny guy always destroys by including himself. He was game for a threesome if we were. My good Christian girl — still very close to the surface — nearly had a heart attack. *How dare he.*

After my girlfriend shot him down, he stared at me and said, "You know, you need to let go or life is going to be really difficult for you." I wish the next words out of my mouth had been *fuck-off* but I was too busy being polite and accommodating because really — I wasn't gay. I just loved my girlfriend and couldn't imagine life without her.

Let go? Here we go again. Let go. Let go of what? My good-standing in evangelical circles was already shot to hell. I left home, graduated from college and was inexorably losing the one person I loved most in the world. He's telling me to let go and have a romp?

Yet even if his body and offer were repulsive, his voice held the tone of prophecy.

I hate when that happens.

However, I've come to learn that the answer doesn't reside in the teacher or ill-suited prophet. It's accepting the lesson that creates a needed shift. It's saying, *okay* and . . . letting go.

You won't catch me in red lipstick or a glossy turban. In fact, the byline of my first business name — Not Your Mother's Tarot — was: *No fancy headdress or smoke machines. Just real Tarot, straight from the gut.* It's embarrassing to refer to myself as a Tarot reader. It's so . . . corny. Or spiritually elitist, depending on the audience.

I have no desire to be a 1-800 psychic. I don't even like people visiting my home. It goes against my very private nature. When that nun offered the Tarot over a decade ago, the cards could have also predicted that I was going to be a mezzo-soprano in the New York City Opera. My reaction would have been the same.

Yeah, right.

Wasn't I supposed to be on a full-fledged Ph.D. track? Be the star English professor at a snooty liberal arts college? Wasn't I going to write the great American memoir and have adoring women crowd around my Sharpie?

Dreams may die hard, but thank God/dess they fall apart. What was pictured as "my future" wouldn't necessarily play out that way, though the essential colors remained.

I have always felt a deep need to offer my gifts in service. That's why the message of the Gospels fit like a handshake; it was the assurance that this life with which God/dess has blessed me would not be wasted if used to help others. Yet my road to being a Tarot reader was anything but easy. I didn't jump into the cards after the retreat and have an amazingly esoteric experience. Tarot was a curiosity piece; a fun game.   Once the deck returned to the nuns, I didn't start studying Tarot until years later. Being a NYC high-school English teacher and grad student demanded every ounce of energy. I grew tired of never having enough money. I adored New York but knew full well the toll she took on my body. My art languished and that killed me.

I've never conformed well to schedules and bosses who cramp my freedom. It was a familiar conundrum: *What next? Out of classroom into the desert? Vermont?* That old Gemini wanderlust stirred heat into my restless city blood.

A dear friend casually dropped a bomb as we noshed on sandwiches one afternoon. She said, "You're a healer. You're going to read cards someday. You don't get it but you are the wounded healer."

Me? A healer? Impossible. More like an angry, bitter 33-year-old ensconced in a life of anthill romances and 40 cats to keep me warm. She was clearly crazy. A healer? My life was a mess. Outwardly responsible and emotionally chaotic otherwise. A healer? Did that mean people would leap from wheelchairs when I touched them? Or was it closer to those Christian counselors who worked so diligently to help me grasp my innate heterosexuality? Or a TV evangelist who strikes people down? Now *that's* more my style.

It was a nice little ego boost . . . for two seconds. I didn't recognize then the prophetic nature of her announcement. Not yet. I wasn't ready to let go of the life I envisioned, though the picture grew murkier by the day.

Vermont slowly started to work her magic in my subconscious but I assumed it would be as a part-timer. Wrong. Vermont wanted all of me. I've learned that *she* chooses a person to live in her beautiful mountains, not the other way around. I moved up during the summer of 2004 and have never looked back.

This state is one of the most magnificent places in the world. Her gentle hills are the supreme antidote for exhausted souls. She's filled with amazing healers and funky, off-grid folk who exude earnest sincerity like Mirabelle, the character played by Claire Danes in *Shopgirl*. When the slutty perfume department girl gives advice on how to trap a man in L.A., Mirabelle thoughtfully shakes her head and says, "I can't do that. I'm from Vermont."

If re-learning how to say *hello* and look people in the eye was an arduous process, so was making friends with my intuition. Tarot kept seeking me out — on cafe tables, bookstore aisles and people literally handing me decks. Others 'mysteriously' wandered into my life to teach me. Or they would simply say, "Good job. Keep going."

Karen was a waitress at Moon Dog Cafe in Chester and casually read for friends using *The Fairies' Oracle*. At first, her kindly nature only made me suspicious — but eventually we began to meet and throw cards. She was so thoughtful and approached the tattered deck like they were old friends. Karen gradually opened my mind to reading Tarot as a profession because it's a way of life in Vermont to work three jobs with one of them doing what you love. A friend sums it up nicely: "We all share equal levels of humiliation here."

Vermont doesn't care about your degrees, your cars or your clothes. A perfect place to be a Tarot reader.

My learning continued. Karen encouraged me to start reading for others but I was not yet ready. I purchased *The Goddess Tarot*. Over and over, I'd throw one card and peer into the tiny book for hours at a time.

Strangers kept saying, "You're a healer," and I started to feel resentful. Healer? That again? Did that mean extra sensitive? Extra crispy? All I could hear was the constant, scornful refrain from my youth: *You're so intense. You're so sensitive.* Being called a healer was too close to those old, worn-out promises that if I prayed enough, loved enough, Jesus would eventually shine down on me. Shine, Jesus, shine.

Learning the Tarot was one thing. Healer? I felt nothing of the sort.

What *was* a healer? The problem lay in the question. Was it Pentecostal preachers and massage therapists? I was often called an old soul. Was that the same as a healer?

Rather than merely struggle, my practical side went to work. It's a fact: if you randomly stick out your hand in Vermont, guaranteed you'll poke an alternative medicine practitioner. This state is rich in healers with quite a few quacks to keep the soup bubbling. I had plenty of psychosomatic symptoms from the City that required attention. Naturopaths, craniosacral and Reiki healers, acupuncturists, old-school therapists; all tended to my wounded soul.

I arrived, I disrobed and asked plenty of questions. The body's innate ability to heal captivated me. Articles were tossed my way on herbal schools and strange men living in the woods. I wasn't ready for a real teacher, which inevitably meant too many half-assed gurus.

Being a hands-on-healer was a potential career, but one major issue stood in the way: I didn't like touching people. I guess that ruled out being a healer?

Mine was a slow and circuitous route into this new world. *New Age* used to mean witches and warlocks and all things Satanic. It also subconsciously included *the gays* and anything I didn't particularly understand.

A year after arriving in Vermont, after all the visits and co-pays, I took a walk one Sunday. It had recently turned 2006 but I was no closer to knowing my place in the Canon of Healers. Massage school and a Reiki class were a wash. My teaching career was nearly over and a great, yawning void loomed. I decided to visit a Spiritualist church in Massachusetts and had an hour to spare before hitting the road. So, I prayed while walking along a snowy trail.

Am I a healer or what, God? What does that mean? I need a sign! Please.

Right on cue, a huge cluster of birds noisily whooshed up into the trees. They may have been grouse or turkeys but I was so startled, I didn't see where they landed. I only said, *That was interesting.* Like a doubting Thomas, this girl needed more. My heart was troubled and a few excited birds weren't going to settle it. I was acutely aware that grouse was "Sacred Spiral" in the *Animal Medicine Cards* — but was in no mood for dancing, thank you. Answers only.

On the slippery slope down, I asked again. *God, am I a healer?*

Birds immediately flew up and away to my left.

Hm. Must have startled them again.

Was it enough? Of course not. I needed a **sign**. I needed the angels to come down and blow a trumpet in my ear.

After a two hour ride to the middle of nowhere, I landed in a town that could have easily been used in the movie, *Deliverance*. I was starving and skidded my way into an icy parking spot surrounded by run-down shacks. If there was a church, I had no idea where to find it. Then I noticed a Spiritualist sign nailed to the side of what looked like a beige hunting lodge. A huge part of my brain yelled, *Screw it! Let's go to Dunkin' Donuts!* but I forced myself to walk to the door, while promising my brain that we'd leave in 30 minutes or less.

Wooden folding chairs were neatly lined up in rows. A canoe hung precariously on the wall above the pulpit with oars scattered around like dull lightning bolts. 50 people or so milled about before the service. I can't stand the appointed greeter, so of course one quickly approached. I was trapped. *Goddamn it.*

I held out my hand like a good girl, then made a beeline for the couch in the back and snuggled down into my heavy wool jacket. Let the show begin.

It did. I couldn't get it out of my head that we were at camp and eager to go swimmin' once the meetin' was over. The guest speaker was female and that pleased me. She was tall, rotund and freshly arrived from out-of-state. She wore a long, braided chain on which hung a gold circle that lay between her cleavage and belly.

After general announcements, the guest speaker approached the podium and asked if any of us wanted a message. Every hand shot up and I couldn't help but notice that a few were held in a jaded sort of way. Bursts of steam from the lasagna on a side table wafted the delicious smell of cheesy sauce under my nose. I love church lunches. The free, olfactory anticipation carried me through many a service back in the day.

I'm number two. She looks at me, points a finger and says, *Do you want a message?* Apparently, I have to not only raise a hand but vocalize my assent before she transmits.

Yes, I say. *I'd like a message.*

She waits a moment, then speaks.

Well, she replies. *You're a healer.*

As I'm reeling but attempt the too-cool-for-school routine, she speaks with the clear tone of someone reciting a shopping list. *Your chakras need support. The spirit of Mother Teresa is with you.* That statement garners some craned necks; hel-*lo.*

She continues. *Some of that illness you carry isn't yours. You're an empath. Protect yourself.* She then turns and gestures to the next needy soul.

Mother Teresa? Does that mean I'll work in Calcutta? Already my mind frantically tries to fill the space created by that mysterious message. *Work with orphans? The dying?* We still have a problem: touching people. Teresa's acute suffering from loving God most certainly doesn't jive with my world view, either.

I did, however, eat two plates of lasagna later while joking with the messenger.

As my heart slowly opened, the work found me. My friend Jacki, owner of the Moon Dog, called one day and said that two women wanted a reading. Was I interested? I hesitated, full of dread. I started walking down the road and heard an inner voice say, *This day is going to change your life*. I was nervous and insecure; my armpits soaking wet. A feather fluttered down and landed right in front of my shoe.

You're all right, the voice seemed to say. *Everything's okay. You're exactly where you need to be.* The thought that they were potentially hot women to date cheered me up.

Date? Nope. They were from Connecticut, dressed to the nines and very jolly. It was another heavenly joke, as I had a particular loathing for Connecticut drivers.

They were gracious after my 45 minute lesson on the history of Tarot. At the end, one woman — I'm sure she was an angel — looked me straight in the eye and said, "My dear, you have a gift."

And so I began.

Like it or lump it, Tarot is a major part of my life and the first step in a lifetime of psychic exploration. I love what I do, even if the name leaves something to be desired.

Normal is overrated, anyway.

My line of work is unusual but the more I grow into it, the less apology needed. It's similar to coming out — which often feels like wearing new skin, so tender and vulnerable.

Plenty of my clients work in professions where I could have easily found success. Stock market. Sales. Professor. They struggle with the same fears of loneliness and lack. Does the outward matter? I suppose to some degree. We want to be respected and recognized for our contributions. Yet at the end of it all, don't we put on our cozy pants and crawl into bed?

Reading cards for a stranger is like walking a marked trail through unfamiliar woods, following the bread crumbs of their soul toward some modicum of truth. It doesn't matter what my clients "do" that gets us there. I've re-introduced thousands — shamans, teachers, doctors, celebrities, lawyers, CEOs, psychics, moms, students and millionaires — to their own inner healer. However, the phrase *reading cards* is a bit of a misnomer. The cards open themselves accordingly. It's similar to the way my oxalis plant unfolds in the morning; a slow, beautiful picture easily missed or taken for granted. I wait for the cards to speak.

My Navajo friend Delyssa says that to call yourself a healer invites laughter within her community. You simply live and people come to the medicine. If you're the real deal, they know where to find it. Am I a healer? It's a strange notion — but Chiron, the wounded healer, does reside in my 4th house.

Is it any surprise that this house represents mother and home, ancestors and endings?

Perhaps it is possible to giggle at my rigidity and not be afraid that God will strike me dead. It's possible to make light of a career which has my devotion. It is possible to have faith, hope and love.

Healer, heal yourself, Jesus once suggested. It's not God, my parents or my ex-lovers' fault. I'm not so frightened, nor am I alone. Each step of faith means another across the valley of desolation — or under the brightest of suns.

It means coming to terms with what I do: reading Tarot cards.

This is my story, this is my song, I sang in church but didn't know either one.

Until now.

Healer. Guide. Artist. Sister. Lesbian. Raven, the messenger of the Goddess.

I will always see Tarot as my friend who opened the door to a world that was simply waiting for me to explore it. No judgment. No shame. Just, *here is your gift and away we go.*

My life is one big, cosmic coyote joke — and I've finally learned to laugh along.

TO BIRTH, TO FLAME
{VIGNETTES OF FIRE}

A BLAST FROM THE REIKI PAST (1998)

My lower back felt like someone tied a slipknot around my muscles and fused them to my spine. I was in delicate, silent agony and pounding concrete City streets didn't help one bit. A trusted friend recommended someone in the Flatiron District who practiced 'Ray-key.' When I asked the meaning, she couldn't quite say.

Just go. She really helped my back. She sorta touches you but doesn't massage.

The name sounded like an exotic noodle. *What's it called again?* I asked.

R-e-i-k-i. Ray-key. And, she said with a big grin, *I think she's a lesbian.*

The magic word. I was always up for meeting a member of my tribe. If things didn't work out with the beautiful scholar, it was wise to line up future possibilities.

Her space was near my gym on 19th street and I booked a session for the following week. My nerves read this as a blind date and tied my back even tighter.

The office was housed in a dark building and a cute, efficient blonde was there to greet me. We squeezed into a tiny room which prominently displayed a picture of another cute, efficient blonde.

I lay on the massage table fully dressed as my prone body folded in on itself like an origami piece. I inwardly reassured her that it was a type of massage.

This is costing us $75. Please relax.

The Reiki person lightly touched my back, her hand lingering on the curved space above my ass and to the right of my tailbone. I expected the warmth of easily flowing blood that comes from massage but only felt an odd and slight embarrassment. As usual. Did I expect my back to unlock like a dusty diary after 20+ years to reveal her pains and sorrowful hopes? *Right.*

The Reiki person then explained the healing process in a whispered monotone.

Don't give me a lesson. Get to what's wrong, then fix it, I inwardly grumped.

After a moment, she spoke again.

"You have a coldness in your lower back. You don't let love in."

Thank God I was on my stomach as my face flamed like a motherfucker. I wanted to throw off the Indian blanket and run, except my back was frozen in place.

I silently burned and hoped her hands started blistering.

I'm paying this Ray-key person to basically tell me I'm frigid? How dare she call me cold! Fucking bitch. Of course I let love in. Wasn't I in a relationship with the beautiful scholar? Didn't I have good friends uptown?

The session was over right then and there. Raven has left the building and luckily without your head on a platter. This time.

My hackles were fully up like the session I had with an acupuncturist who neglected to remove two needles in my shoulder while tiding up a domestic dispute over the phone. No apology *and* she expected her outrageous fee! I was a coward to not call her out. Nor did I with the

Reiki person. I lodged a complaint with my friend but she was simply flabbergasted. The Reiki person did amazing things to her body.

Maybe I *was* cold. Maybe I didn't let love in.

It was all a crock of shit, anyway.

Ray-key. What a joke.

MY ANGER WEARS A BLACK HOODIE

I want to be a kinder, more peaceful person. I do. It's such an appealing idea. Thich Nhat Hanh in his economically titled book, *Anger*, suggests embracing rage like a mother comforting her baby.

Now is the ideal time: my latest ex helpfully shares that I have anger issues before yelling, "Fuck off!" and slamming down the phone.

The happily-ever-after quickly turns to sitting shiva. Lust, Insecurity, Vulnerability and Happiness already circle up by the fire, attempting to thaw out. This time, I invite Anger but she doesn't even RSVP. She just shoots over with a trunk full of explosives.

Giddy up, little soldier.

I envision a looming presence and am startled when a 4' 11" gansta covered head to toe in a skull-stamped black hoodie swaggers up. She stops right at the edge of the Welcome mat. The others nervously ignore her. She's crashed many a party and after three decades, they are finished with her antics.

Anger stands there like a concrete pillar; doesn't show her face or let me take her hoodie. She is goddamn for sure not going to sit until she goddamn well pleases. Still, it's toasty inside and she looks tired of being left out in the cold. There's some old beef with Vulnerability but she isn't here for a throwdown. Not yet. More pressing matters press.

Happiness and Insecurity sip Manhattans and chat away in an effort to regain their feminine graces, while Lust simply pouts in a corner. It's been a tough week for all after losing a sultry summer romance that offered regular doses of wild sex. Anger is ready to rumble and pissed that we aren't rushing to the safety deposit box to grasp the well-worn *Scorched Earth Policy*. Not that it is needed. We know it by heart.

Though her eyes are cast down, I feel a bubbling excitement lengthening her spine. Her thoughts thrust out like shiny swords.

Payback time. What did that bitch say? Fuck off? Ha. Anger? She ain't seen nothin' yet. We filter everything through a defensive shield? Smart cookie. Not too in touch with her own issues. When I'm done with her, Anger mumbles, *she'll feel every wounded piece of herself. Call it my special trigger-point therapy.*

The more I tune into my nemesis, the more my blood pulses. That same thrilling rush of adrenaline.

Maybe this is life, I think. *Tell the truth. Nothing held back. Fuck it. Anger and I do so well together. Our exs may not like us but they sure as hell remember us.*

Bubble, bubble, toil and trouble.

Love, the Goddess, glows with extra wattage in the periphery. I roll my eyes at her.

Gimme a break. I know your game. You want me to feel all empathetic. "Let go". Be compassionate 'n shit. Remember "the good". Realize "the purpose" of our time together. Right. Here we are, processing another broken heart. Same old shit. Same old place. Bitter and hopeless. I'm done with soft.

Glow, glow, glow.

Anger pushes, pushes, pushes to call back, pick up a pen, do *something* for fuck's sake!

Let's go! Are we going to fucking let her get away with that fucking shit? No one talks to us like that! What the FUCK are you doing sitting there? Don't pay attention to Love!

This time, I hesitate. The wearisome toll that Anger demands tilts the scales. I want us to finally experience something that is a rarity in our world.

Peace.

I offer her a drink — but am met with a huffy refusal.

She does, however, step over the threshold.

GOOD CHRISTIAN GIRLS

When I was a good Christian girl in a good Christian college, there was an evil place that we feared, directly in the heart of our tiny river town. It seethed with witches, New-Agers and assorted unsaved folk. An enormous white arrow encircled the brick wall, helpfully pointing south.

It was the metaphysical bookshop in the basement of the health food store. No surprise that the depths of hell hid beneath rotting boxes of produce.

It terrified but ennobled a small band of Christians known as the "prayer warriors". I was one of them. Our mission was to save those patronizing the bookshop by rapidly putting it out of business.

The strategy?

We'd circle the building, hands interlocked. The strength of the Lord was before, in and around us. We'd pray for Truth to shine a light in the darkness.

We'd claim it for the Lord.

I was, as usual, uncertain about the method — but my college had the strongest prayer circle in town. Our gospel teams were known far and wide. One store would be a piece of cake.

Or so we thought.

The smarter plan would have been to create a prayer chain that encircled the whole town but in the end, our faith was weak. Our prayers unheard. Clearly, the former monk who ran the place had

more sway with God . . . or the Devil. Decades on, the shop —
which is now twice the size of the original — continues to share an
uneasy peace with the college on the hill.

I laugh at these memories. What is it with the need to save others?
Isn't there enough in our own lives to fortify, nourish and grow? Live
by example. Do no harm.

Prayer warriors. God's eternal defenders. Onward, Christian soldiers.
The hero gene simmering beneath the surface. Save the day. Rescue
the maiden. Kill the bad guy and hear God say, "Well done, my good
and faithful servant." To have a purpose . . . and then fulfill it.

Intensity of focus in the guise of goodness can so easily turn sour.
My way or the highway, baby.

Does co-existence even exist?

Letting people live the way they wish and do no harm.

Do no harm. That's the clincher.

Who am I to tell someone that they need to be healed? Saved?

Maybe the cat lady likes her life with 45 cats. Maybe the drunk enjoys
heckling women. Maybe the couch potatoes want to lard away their
days watching reality TV.

That's their choice. Healing only works when someone is willing to
be healed. That doesn't imply brokenness. It means all of the ways
we say no to life. All of the ways we betray our dreams on a daily
basis. All of the ways we could have evolved through difficult times,
healing the disconnect from our own goodness.

Life constantly provides options to be lighter and easier while on this stage. That's why proselytizing rarely works. We are responsible for waking ourselves up.

Many clients ask, "Do you think we're headed for great disaster in 2012?"

It's up to us. What I do know is that pride has always limited the human race. The need to save becomes the need to conquer. To encircle in the name of the Lord. To destroy, rebuild and repeat. Ad nauseam.

I wanted to "bridge the gap" when I was a good Christian. Help the lost find freedom and peace through Christ. What was a pure desire for healing became pure distraction. Fear. Arrogance. To be as Christian as possible, which often meant being the loudest groaner in a prayer circle. My focus — the perfectionist never satisfied — was to guide souls to salvation. The poorer, the better.

The irony, of course, was that my life languished in purgatory at my good Christian college. I didn't understand then that truth is an entrance into the Great Mysteries. That God is beyond our boxes while at the same time existing within.

That no one is greater than another.

To bridge the gaps in our own understanding.

To offer the greatest goodness to our own beings.

To love our self like we love God/dess and our neighbor.

Maybe this is the path to salvation.

WHERE I'VE DONE IT

I've done it in every kind of place. Tiny cafes in nowhere Vermont. Chain restaurants where everyone crowds the bar, warbling and screaming. On a street festival table. A ratty picnic bench in the middle of a Floridian town square while fearing I'd be dragged off at any moment. My house. Their house. Mansions. Cute little Capes. Salt caves. Smack down on the edge of a baseball field. Over the phone. Under trees. Video Skype. In my car — front and back seats. Parking lots. A creepy concrete basement filled with dusty shit. Birthday parties. Over a gigantic salad.

That's the beauty of my work. Reading Tarot provides enviable flexibility. No office space needed. No rent to be paid. A computer, phone, two feet and my maroon bag of tricks. I'm good.

I quickly learned to become master of my domain, however. No more musty basement sessions with potential Satanists. No more walking disturbed. No more unfamiliar houses unless they belong to returning clients. Absolutely no smoking around the cards. No lazy drunks full of excuses. No clients who bitch about my prices.

They can find another Tarot reader. There are plenty in the metaphysical sea.

It's good to be selective. It's wise to be discerning. It's my time and energy, after all.

The cards ask for the same love and respect, wherever you happen to do it.

NICHES ARE FOR WISHES

"What are you?"

I've been hearing that question since birth.

Followed by, "What do you do?"

Though the need to categorize is understandable, I've never had a clear response. The ancient Gemini conundrum: there's always more than one answer.

Which comes to this idea of niches. *What's your niche? Niche? That's so last year. What's your micro-niche?*

Niche. It's a word often thrown around in my social media circles.

I don't care for it.

Why? It's limiting. And I hate cages of any kind.

When I started this work, people would ask, "What is it exactly that you do?"

I'd answer, "I'm a Tarot reader."

Which I never cared for. Guess why? Too limiting.

I needed a niche. I couldn't say, "I'm a healer". What did that mean?

The cards gave me a place. I started to be "known" — and chafed under the title. It's kind of ironic since my radio show was called . . . *Tarot Talk.*

Many of my clients are healers who feel the pressure of finding a niche, even within their chosen modality.

My advice? Don't drive yourself crazy with this stuff. Niches are overrated.

You could have the fanciest website in the world. Thousands of followers on social media. Line up your degrees from here to the garage. Have a kick-ass bio. Very good things.

Yet it all ends up being pretty shallow if potential clients don't essentially and inherently trust you.

Once they do, they don't care about your title. They want the mutual healing that comes from your time together. They want to feel the hope and excitement that dances in their soul after speaking with you.

As my fellow Taroist Bonnie Cehovet advises: "Understanding your niche is well worth the effort. Having it define you is a problem."

During my time wintering in Florida, I'd do little bullshit readings at a picnic table in town. I'd meet all types: from homeless to multi-millionaires who'd ask the same questions. A sketchy guy started lurking around. He was a cross between a hit man and a burned out bass player with a Bruce Springsteen underbite. However, I've done this work long enough to know that if I'm uncomfortable, more than likely s/he is my teacher of the moment — and close attention is required.

I did a reading for him, then he casually pulled out a worn deck. *Ah. That's who you are, sketchy guy. A fellow reader.* He offered one in return.

Sure enough, we were mutually impressed — though his reading seemed a little out there, to be honest. Me, in Israel?

I'd see him around town and he'd always call me "Isis". Right before heading north and to the subsequent upheaval of my mom's death, he said, "I want to do a reading before you leave, Isis. Meet me in the park."

He read my cards and said that money would soon arrive as I was penniless at the time. Then he paused. "You need to know something," he said. "You're a healer. That's it. No bullshit titles — Tarot reader this, medium that. A healer. Period. Don't get caught up in the other stuff."

That was absolutely the best lesson I've ever learned about niches.

Don't stress a niche. When people trust you, you've got it all.

THE POWER OF ONE

1

1:01

1:11

11:11

1.1.11

1.11.11

11.1.11

11.11.11

Make a wish.

Begin.

THE EVERYDAY MAGICIAN

Long before Harry Potter and the Tarot, my first real understanding of a magician was a man who horrifyingly sawed a woman in half and then healed her. He also pulled a rabbit out of a hat, but that wasn't as impressive. I learned that the Magician created something out of thin air. What was intangible to us was meat and potatoes to him.

The beauty of a Tarot card like I Magician is that it can't be completely nailed down. It's a flexible framework, similar to adding layers over a beautiful painting which serve to enhance the final work. The Magician takes the contrary courage of the Fool and steps into her reality. This determined power births from the connection that we have to the 4 elements: Fire, Air, Water, Earth.

How it works? Try explaining that.

The magician/shaman of old was able to envision the warring ships at sea while the Indians only focused on small boats invading their shores. The Magician actively sees the larger picture even when no one believes them.

No one plays harder with what we consider an illusion than the Magician. And no one guards their secrets more obsessively. The Magician does not let "reality" run the show.

How does this translate to daily life, which turns from tedious to sparkling in a moment?

Ask yourself: *do I believe in magic?* If you can honestly say yes, move on to #2. Otherwise, watch the Wonder Twins. Practice their moves.

- Study the 4 elements and deeply understand them. This means sensory experience, not mere intellect. Feet in mud, walking in rain, observing insects, seeing how the larger world operates and your place in it.

- Know that magic hovers around the mundane, waiting to be recognized.

- Remember that your thoughts — what you visualize — have great power to shape your reality. As do your words.

- You control the ON/OFF button of your power. Not your parents, pastor, lover or kids. You. Be wise about it. No one drains a Magician faster than a naysayer.

- Call upon and use the elements. This is where gemstones are your friend. They hold all of the elements within their being. Stones grant an easy and ancient entrance to the world of magic.

These are a few examples of how gemstones can assist you:

- Need energy/fire? Red Carnelian.

- Need clarity/air? Selenite, a beautiful worker bee stone. Onyx.

- Need an open heart/water? Jasper. Adventurine. Any green stone.

- Need negativity banished/earth? Obsidian, Healer's gold.Hematite.

The Magician reminds us: as above, so below. Once we understand that we are creators rather than passive participants, that our actions weave into the fabric of eternity, it provides us with a wider vision than the 24/7 survival mode.

That's the everyday gift of the Magician.

I'LL TAKE AN ORDER OF PURPOSE . . . OR NOT.

Age is a construct. Actually, the entire show is a construct.

Nevertheless, the numbers keep changing in May. Numbers, numbers.

Over my cup of coffee this morning, I thought back to the trinkets of my 20s and the distressful search for what would *make me happy*. I was always straddling the line of too little debauch and not enough holiness. There had to be meaning in everything or it was worthless.

Whenever I flung out my net, a boatload of rusty cans rattled back. No girlfriend completely satisfied. I adored the City but longed for the country — and vice-versa. A job? I hated the 9-5. Nope, not followin' the man — though most of my bosses were female. I'd constantly negotiate less hours and was fortunate enough to have a long-suffering friend who was also a big wig publishing exec and tolerated my fickleness.

I'd stroll into those 6th Avenue offices in my beat-up combat boots with an eye firmly on the clock, suffering another slow death by cubicle. There's truly nothing worse than attempting to find a sliver of sunlight between the high-rises of Midtown.

In my frenzy to locate peace — that transient calm — I wouldn't have recognized Life if she sat on my lap in a miniskirt and a pair of hot Frye boots.

That's the thing about Life. She provides us with plenty of grace. She allows the rumspringa of our souls, if you will. The movement of my 20s literally kept me alive. Instead of drugs, I bought a motorcycle. I moved in and out of the City on a whim, dating plenty of women wherever I landed. I like to think that my older self — that wiser being — hovered protectively over my restless soul.

I wanted to be a writer. A professor. Make a killing in the stock market. Make a name for myself. Wander cross-country.

And beauty? Beauty was everywhere . . . just out of reach. The God from long ago existed in another universe.

Plenty of trinkets and time to sort through the worth of them. The biggest? I had to decide if I really liked that girl who always shadowed: me. There were hellish moments when I wished to call out, "Check, please!" but that steel rod spine kept walking — because that is what she does. Rise, and walk.

The reason? Purpose. I sure as hell wasn't going exit stage left before grabbing onto it. Fulfillment was another matter.

During my fervent attempts at Christianity, my purpose was one thing: love God. I'd stand on the edge of a rocky cliff high in the mountains during an exquisite sunset and call out. I needed to feel God.

I didn't — because "God" was beyond that beauty. Above, out there, distant. The pallet of colors, flowery fields, the birds calling goodnight were trinkets that led to God's existence. Except it was a hijacked fairy tale where a wicked animal ate the crumbs right before I found God's house.

Or maybe God kept changing the arrow signs in the maze and I circled back to the cliff's edge, peering out with earnest eyes. Waiting. Always waiting.

Even in the cities — Portland, Denver, my beloved New York — I called out for God. The greatest purpose? Unfulfilled. In the beauty of a naked woman standing before me, I called out to God. Unfulfilled.

In my search for meaning, I was making a god of it. Expecting the deity to pronounce, "You must do this and this to equal a meaningful life. You must be called _____ and work to your fullest ability. Then and only then, will I grant entrance."

Maybe after all that wandering, my purpose is to simply be.

That's not enough, right? There must be more.

Stay with me here.

To enjoy. To revel. Yes, it bears repeating: have a passionate love affair with this form we carry. That's enough purpose for an entire life. In this form is the shape of God, not the "God-shaped void".

It's easy to get entangled in *having a purpose* — show up, dress the part, wear scuffed combat boots, publish a book or not, chase God — only to find ourselves locked up in a label.

Labels are nice. They define, organize, calm. Gemini. Healer. Lesbian. Female. I can appreciate brevity and page-turners. However, labels + purpose are a deadly combo if we don't like ourselves. If we can't find a way to deeply appreciate this life, we will constantly fool ourselves into doing battle with a supposed shadow or distant God — when the truth is that we just can't stand the person in the mirror.

For today, drop the idea of having a purpose.

Lessen the need for a label to slap on and carry through life.

Appreciate yourself a little bit more.

Because in the end — who are we, really?

We are who we are and we are here because we are here.

Isn't that enough?

THE MUSIC OF THE SPHERES

Many clients ask: "Raven, I have so much creative energy inside. How do I use it? Where do I direct it? I don't have a clue!"

In my own artistic life and overall search for meaning, the answer is far more simple than I am willing to admit.

Art has to be hard, right? The suffering, starving, depressed artist?

Yeah. That worked for my 20s. Add combat boots and motorcycle. Mix.

To use that beautiful energy is to say *yes* to it. To open a space in your head and heart through which that fiery creativity can flow.

How to make space? Allow stillness. Practice receiving. Do this enough so your Muse trusts that you are present for her gift.

The angels don't require direction; only permission to flow through us.

Every great work of art is a direct channeling of the Divine. It is infused with the music of the spheres. It only waits to be granted entrance. Get this: it doesn't stop flowing if we don't get it right the first time. We need to be willing to start and stop and start again.

That's the beauty of perfection: it's perfectly malleable.

Often the idea of *artist* or *creativity* is fused to what is commonly seen as "art": writing, painting, photography, etc. Those are simply a few of the innumerable ways that the original Artist can create with us.

How can we open to this movement? It's the passion that arises when you sing, offer a loving hand, put pen to paper, make love with your full self. It's listening to the suffering that urgently asks for liberation. It's the goosebumps of *just right*.

Find your unique way. Then find another. And another. It's the path of the true artist.

The objective?

Healing.

The process?

Healing.

The result?

Healing.

Always healing.

CHASING UTOPIAS

It's easy to get caught up in chasing utopias. Such a pretty net. Ethereally thin. It's like the heaven of my youth = the ultimate utopia. When life crunched down, there was always that golden promise just beyond my fingertips. Live a good life on this sinful planet, believe in Jesus and soon you'll reach those pearly gates to collect your reward for toughing it out.

It was a fabulous goal. Those mansions in the sky weren't the exciting part — it was the freedom from pain. The healing of my broken heart. The love I didn't feel when everyone told me that *yes, Jesus loves me*. Or not.

There are so many utopias born out of the desire to end suffering. The heated seats. The little place in the country. A winning Powerball ticket. A happy relationship — or leaving the one you despise. Ditching a dreadful job or citizenship. A fat 401K.

But if not now, when?

If today doesn't satisfy, will a warm butt in January make it better?

I spent a good 15 years chasing utopias. The perfect place to live. The best coffee. The most peaceful of forests. Beautiful women, one after the other.

Sometimes the landing was blissful.

Sometimes I raced out of there so fast, no one knew my name.

That's the thing about utopias. They shift as we shift. Change as we grow. And they are always — tantalizingly — out of reach.

Why? Because they are a gorgeous illusion.

Use them at will. Take what you need from yearning — but don't built a house there.

If not now, when?

TO MOVE, TO HOPE, TO DREAM

Moving. I'm an expert at it.

I have the unending morass of my childhood to thank for planting a seed of desperation to break free and breathe. What kept me alive? A battered Appalachian Trail Guide and a tiny emergency survival kit. I promised myself that I'd hike the entire AT once I left home for good.

Instead, I moved all over the U.S. after college — Cape Cod, Colorado, Jersey City, NYC, Hudson river towns, Portland (West Coast version), Las Vegas, Florida, Vermont.

If I had a hankering for a certain state, I'd stuff my hatchback and go. This was after months of silent contemplation — but always made the trip look like I was doing it on the fly.

Some of the moves were just to move. Some for love. Some were the *fuck you, you'll miss me* tire skids. A memorable one was in the dead of the night, a 350 Honda hitched to my car with a mewking kitten in the front seat. A few were purely economical. A couple were the lick-my-wounds kind.

Most of them were to unknown places. There was so much pleasure in starting fresh, building a life and finding my way. I needed to prove something: to my perfectionist father and the emerging woman. I needed to learn about courage, over and over again.

This was freedom to me.

At times I rented spaces simply because they were beautiful, like the Fort Collins stained glass castle on Mulberry Street. Or the crumbling Highland Falls Victorian with curved bay windows overlooking the Hudson. I liked imagining the stories of the people who lived there. Other places I couldn't leave quick enough, like the Jersey City railroad apartment owned by crackhead landlords or the beige nightmare Las Vegas condo that only highlighted the bitter, selfish and sad woman I had become.

Moving? It's how I roll. Am I tired? Yes. A part of me would love a home. But what *is* home? Home is anywhere I go. Anywhere my cats are. Where my art hangs. Where my car rests in the driveway. Wherever birds flutter around.

Home is wherever I am.

This adaptability has served me well in life but every time I move, I'm nervous. Every time. You'd think I would be more than used to it by now. I'm often terrified but outwardly confident. I easily manifest lovely places but moving isn't as thrilling as it once was. It's kind of a pain in the ass. The cats are old. I'm sick of piling shit in the car. The same questions haunt: can I afford it? What if I'm lonely? What if I never stop moving?

Moving is complicated. Risky. And still, the thrill.

Life beckons. And I've never been able to resist her call. When my work is done, I move on. Vermont continually surprises me. I've been here seven years, six longer than planned. The dreadful cold SO does not suit my temperament — but I'm in love with the place. She has taught me the merit of staying put long enough to build a community. I love her while knowing that in not-too-distant future, I will head on down that familiar highway.

Moving brings excitement. A freshness. It encourages expansion. It brings new roads, new trails, new faces. Where's the best coffee? Ooh, I haven't seen that stand of trees before. What's around that curve? I love to put my particular stamp on every place.

Yes, we can surely view the same landscape with new vision — but unexplored territories are where I thrive.

I never did trace the entire AT. But thank heavens for that map and the dream of 2,000 miles carrying me away from home. It saved my life. It helped me escape. It made me happy to know that no matter where I was at the time, there were always new places that whispered my name, waiting for my arrival.

AS THE FIRE WANES IN A FIERY WOMAN

Some of my female clients are full of fire. I call them the *swing from the chandelier* types. Doesn't matter the age; sparks trail behind them. Usually they are Aries women. Whatever their sign, they are most certainly fiery women.

Which makes it frustrating to see when they are attached to a dud of a relationship. Or simply a dud. Cheater dud, angry dud, couch potato dud that they surround with their impossibly fierce, loyal love.

Sometimes I want to leap up and say, "Get out! Leave! Start fresh! What are you doing? Have you forgotten that you're FIRE?!"

They'd just laugh and say, *I know, Raven* while dreaming up more excuses as to why they'll stay. Failure is not an option for them.

The heart is like a turtle. She will go to wherever she is going on her peculiar timetable, no matter how the mouth or brain try to convince otherwise. No sooner.

Take my advice. Don't even try to persuade a fiery woman.

One of two things happen when a fiery woman is betrayed:

a) the life force peters out.

b) they immediately start plotting a murder.

Good luck finding any middle ground.

Their optimistic nature can't hide a deep wound but an incredible strength keeps shouting, *Live! Live!*

How well? How brightly?

I said to one fiery client, *You are not your partner's healer. Catalyst, maybe. But you are not meant to solve the riddle of their anger.*

Tread carefully with fiery women. They are very strong, like it direct and rarely resist a challenge. Throw a lifelong conundrum at them and they'll have the solution plus ten different options by morning.

When they come to me in pain, they need to be reminded of their power. They need to give themselves permission to be strong again. They need to feel the fresh air of freedom and possibility on their faces.

What they don't need is a solution. Trust me on that. They already know.

So whatever you say, say it gently.

DEATH, THE DEVIL
AND A LITTLE THING CALLED SETTLE

We can always blindly hope for perfection.

Or we can finally recognize the difference between compromise and settling.

Ever come across these scenarios?

Toil in a loathsome job rather than follow your heart's desire?

Saying "I do" even though you don't — to please everyone else?

Remain frozen in a relationship that has long passed its expiration date?

Stay stuck in a location because it's easier than leaping into the unknown?

Run away from someone because you're afraid of losing your "freedom"?

Tolerate a partner's abuse/self-absorption because it's better than being alone?

Stay in a church whose doctrines turn your stomach but you're afraid of being ostracized by the flock?

To settle is to sacrifice your beautiful life on the altar of less-than-ideal and hope that someday it gets better.

It won't.

Settling is to make melancholy your bedmate while lying to yourself every day. To tuck your inner knowledge into a self-help book that lays forgotten in a pile of self-help books.

To compromise is to work with discomfort until it is transformed. Compromise is never accepting less in regards to the long-term. It's allowing expansion. To decide to leave or stay in a relationship / job / ideology — and then do it. It's not making the temporary reprieve of compromise an eternal excuse (my kids, sick partner, aging parents, pastor, bank account is why I can't change anything.)

This is where XIII Death in the Tarot comes to your aid.

Death means letting it die.

Death: the ultimate transformer of an intuitive couch potato.

Transformation comes in many disguises but intuition *always* marks the stage with blindingly white tape. She is your fiercest, most loyal guide if you let her be (I prefer "her" rather than "it" in deference to II High Priestess, but intuition encompasses the various me-s).

That's the thing about intuition — it's very sane. It's not all poprockets and wands here. It's using what you've got to improve your life. Awakening to the ever-present moment, no matter how shitty it is.

Does a rose get more beautiful as it unfolds?

Or do we open to the all-that-is beauty right in front of us?

The rose eventually dies. It must. It must make way for the perfection to come.

See the beauty of the life you desire vs. the life you are living right now as a great gift of contrast. That squirmy, uncomfortable, "God. I am NOT happy."

Intuition is your best friend. She'll say, "Girl, why ride the crazy train? Let's take a stroll and repair those broken fences. Let's work on that dignity piece. You are all-that, so why accept anything less?"

However, intuition is no fool. She'll nudge when settle is wearing out its welcome — but she's no eardrum blaster.

The next step is my responsibility.

So much can be lost in pure laziness. Zoning out. TV. Playing games with ourselves and others. Avoiding pain. Staring freedom down and saying, "Really. What's the use?"

This is where XV Devil — which I consider the darkest card of the Tarot — offers liberation or lockdown.

The Devil's in the details? Nah. The Devil is in the settling. He'll say, "That's all you want in life? You got it, sweetheart. I'm happy to oblige." If you look closely at the card, the chains can easily slip off the couple in bondage. The Devil isn't holding them back. They are.

Compromise, as I well know, isn't a bed of roses. It is one big pain in the ass.

At the very least, we *feel*. That opens the power of the gut which initiates us into the Great Awakening.

Our own.

AS ABOVE, SO BELOW

Everyone is capable of magic.

Magic is everywhere and particularly brilliant in spring. Readily harnessed and wholly elusive. Over, beyond and in us.

Your body may become ill or carry a nameless anxiety around this time of year. The clearing of lungs, heart, skin, lovers. You may find her going through tremendous emotion. You may feel flutters of unexpected joy.

Follow where she leads. Honor her movements. Prepare for birth.

Not surprisingly, it's also one of the busiest seasons for me. Midwifery time.

Magic. Spring. Both must be approached with respect and awe. It's easy to glory over the crocuses — and yes, how lovely. However, primal forces lie right behind the delicate beauty. The pulsing. The thrumming. Rushing winds. Cracking rivers. The indomitable push of the rampant new through ancient waters.

This is magic. As above, so below. The power that surrounds is the power within. An eternal mystery hides in the redundancy of cycles. The Earth reflects our internal movement — and shifts in ways that are completely her own. She is the eternal Mother.

Spring welcomes eternal life. She opens her treasures to those who approach with love. As a result, we tap a direct line into those birthing forces. The life blood of eternity.

Nature is here to teach us — if we regard her as both Mother and friend. It can be as simple as sinking your fingers into warm, fresh mud. Being drenched in moonlight. Mapping the path of birds. Feeling the electric charge of the earth soaking into your feet, body and out through your fingertips. Allowing your self to completely heal. Believing that you can.

It's acknowledging this power, then using it wisely.

I recently watched a documentary that referred to Mother Nature as a "mean old biddy". This is an unfortunate attitude that separates us from magic. It takes the Empress — the symbol of fertility in the Tarot — and reduces her to a vengeful old maid, arbitrarily meting out destruction in response to her barren womb.

It's a learned, tragic disconnect to the Mother.

Magic is very simple when done as a daily practice. The more we become conscious of our attitudes toward the Earth and her cycles, the clearer we understand that we are either creators or destroyers.

Spring offers us the gift of re-birth. The Vernal Equinox is the astrological New Year, as the zodiac begins in Aries. It's a mutual healing. A new start.

That the power of magic. That is the power of spring.

Happy New Year.

WHEN THE HEART ANSWERS

I asked my heart what she wanted this morning. Truly.

A word to the wise: only ask your heart if you're ready for an answer. Because she will. It may take time, but she will. Again and again and again.

As I sat in my dreaming chair — a weathered Adirondack overlooking the mountains — and sipped green tea, I was the ideal picture of crunchy happiness. I waited.

It didn't take long. The usual suspects came first. *Love. A girlfriend. An easy flow. A rockin' business.*

While they were nice answers, I grew suspicious. It was sounding all too familiar. That voice was the spokeswoman of a chatty Gemini mind. But I patiently listened until she was through, went inside and put on my bathing suit. Then I drove down to the river.

As soon as my feet touched water, that's when my heart opened up. And did she speak.

We're not talking gentle water here. We're talking fire. The movement of flame.

When my heart answered, it was completely different from the plans laid out for the coming year. Those plans were good. Adult plans. In all fairness, they had me excited. Not mindblowingly excited, but excited enough.

No. Not yet. Not enough. Or maybe after, said my heart.

My heart isn't timid. She's more like a queen tapping her foot, waiting to be heard. She doesn't waste time on half-assed attention.

What then did my queen command?

Travel. Drive. Travel. No rent. Less rent. Visit ashrams/retreats and move on. Sing kirtan to my heart's content. Be open to meeting strangers and feel the magic of that fleeting or lasting connection. Keep using my gifts in different venues. Drive. Visit. Find a cabin and write. Crash with friends for a day or two. Drink really good coffee. Go south. Be warm, wherever the wind takes me. Stay in VT. Come back to VT. Or not.

There's usually a defined plan before any big moves, though I'm often seen as a free spirit. Little do they know how long I negotiate with my mercurial escape routes. Change exhilarates and terrifies me.

I've learned over the years that peace comes from greeting my internal landscape with as much enthusiasm as I have for the actual road. *Place* really doesn't matter. Following the cycles of my heart — well, there's the clincher. Good thing it's usually in the fall. Seasons fitting like hair color to names.

Of course, my mind had to butt right in with its overwrought largesse of wisdom. "Well, that's fine and good but who's going to take care of the cats? What about clients? What about staying in place? This is why you don't have a girlfriend. Money? Cats?

My heart sat this one out, watching the mental volley with amusement. She knew that something had sparked.

It was only a matter of time before we flamed.

CHILDBIRTH SANS CHILDREN

I've given birth plenty of times. Just not through my womb.

My words birth from mind, fingers, voice. They are my little seeds who wait for the consummate moment to blossom and ripen.

Yes. It is the Empress energy that courses in me. It's taken a very long time for us to fully merge. She is the great Nurturer, the life giver. The ultimate woman. The one who embraces skin and bones and sex.

The flesh and bone kind? Baby fever? Nah. Not for me.

I held the sweetest little one as her mother stood nearby with an expectant look.

Oh, I've seen it plenty of times before.

She finally spoke. "And . . . nothing?"

"Nothing. Sorry." I replied, handing back the kid. "But she's a great baby. A old soul."

My lack of baby fever shocks more than a few mothers. Is a genetic defect to blame when my heart doesn't fill with longing at the sight of a stroller? In fact, I immediately leave the room when a kid starts to wail.

However, my womb is fertile and rich. I can sense children waiting to be born; at least two. The greatest irony is that even at 41, I could very easily give birth.

Yet I've said a firm *no*. Do those eager spirits understand? Do they choose another mother? Another vessel? Will I meet them down the eternal road?

It's all the more puzzling when desperate women who long to be pregnant book a session with me — a happily childless woman with a fertile womb.

They've given up hope. Resigned themselves to a childless life. Still, they call for their children through the cards. I feel their womb crying. No other love can erase this urging of the soul. I flow gently around these women because my heart is filled with love and sorrow.

Sometimes I wish I didn't feel as much as I do.

I understand the deep need of seeing one's face reflected. But a session can quickly turn awkward when a client dismisses the idea of adoption. Like it's the day-old loaf of bread. Useful but unappetizing. Sure to bring up the trigger of my birth. All of the questions that remain in the shadow of my lost mother.

Do you want me?

No. Obviously not.

Numerous reasons. Perfectly understandable. You did the best you could with the best you had at the time.

Or so we like to say.

Let's finally speak the truth. You didn't want me. There's another family as evidence.

You didn't want to redefine, explain, transform.

You walked as far as you could, then returned home with a body that held the remembrance of me.

And if there are no children to speak of, what then?

How much of this is born from pure desire?

How much of this is ego unwilling to die?

If I disappear, who am I then?

When my mother disappears, who am I then?

As women, this life holds such promise for us. What happens when we spend the majority seeking our lost children? Our lost mothers?

When we call out: *Do you want me?*

And the clear answer that returns from the emptiness: *No. Obviously not.*

What then? How do we create from such a silence?

Where do we go with raw anger? Grief?

No one understands.

It is your child you seek.

Is it?

Is it you?

Is it you who seeks?

Is it you,

you seek?

STEPS TO BEING A POWERFUL WOMAN

- Don't merely say that you are powerful. Own it.

- Say no. Often. Mean it.

- Look men directly in the eye and tell the truth. Start with yourself.

- Appreciate your body in every facet of aging. Stop telling her she isn't good enough.

- Practice shoulder opening exercises. Nothing says 'queen' like an upright carriage.

- Find ways to love yourself. Learn to speak kindly. This is the key to everything.

- You are not your rape. You are not your abuse. You are a powerful woman.

- Learn the power of *yoni*. She rules the world. Your yoni's voice may be a whisper. But oh, the secrets she could tell.

- Sacrifice your sacrificial self on the altar. Finally. The Old Testament times are over. God isn't asking for your firstborn. Stop asking for permission to be here. Be here.

- You came with a plan, and you are perfect in that plan. By the way, that plan has a built-in elastic waistband.

- Speak confidently. Your life is not held in a question mark.

- Know when to listen.

- Tell your breasts how fabulous they are, how nurturing — even if they sag or are no longer attached to your body. They are still yours — and they are beautiful.

- Throw out your modern iron maidens.

- Listen to birds. Step away from your computer. See the sky. Don't forget Nature.

- Wise women tell tales. Own your story. Truth will follow you anywhere.

- You are not your father's disappointment. Step out of the glare.

- Old lovers are still your mirror. It's not about letting go. It's learning how to gaze deeply, then place the mirror back in the drawer.

- Do battle with your inner tyrant. Tell her/him that they are no longer welcome. Know that they may return — but you hold the keys to entrance.

- Find a way to understand the word *contentment*.

- Remember the boy who said you were ugly? He lied.

- Memorize a line of poetry, kirtan, a lover's letter. Carry it like a flashlight in the dark.

- No one is below you. Or above you. Every job is valuable. Every heart is vulnerable. Learn to see through illusion.

- Life can be bite-sized. Discover what you can handle and stop there. No pain, no gain is bullshit.

- Embrace your intuition. She is your most trusted ally. If you have forgotten her, woo her back. Believe again. Believe.

- Everyone begins as a woman. Everyone. Let that comfort you.

- Even when there is no hope, your life will continue. It can't help but do so.

- Death is the most misunderstood blessing in the Universe. Embrace your Crone. She is the one who guides you into the Mysteries.

- Find your female god within. Bring her back. Shine the light.

- For every moment of grace, there is suffering. Love guarantees nothing but presence.

- The greatest tenderness and most ruthless protector births from a self-aware woman.

- Don't wait for others to recognize your power. Just use it.

- Allow yourself the space and grace to fuck up.

- Know when to step back and allow another woman to step ahead.

- If you can't trust your intuition, save your money and don't go to a psychic.

- Freedom isn't with the next lover or running to some tropical island. Freedom is looking yourself straight in the eye at your darkest moment — and still saying *yes*.

- Our moon is one of our greatest times of power. Once you wrap your head around this koan, you'll understand why men have sought to suppress us for eons.

- Women will rule the world once we allow ourselves to rule the world. Be part of the shift.

- Bring yourself into alignment with your present purpose. All of your previous goals, failures and flounderings have brought you to this moment. Perfectly.

- Deal with your pain. It doesn't simply free you — it liberates the women to come. Set them free.

REIKI LOVE

One of the greatest gifts of Reiki is its breathtaking power to restore. A friend with an unexpected health issue remembered that I did hands-on healing and booked a session. He's a burly Vermont carpenter. Not the first person you'd think would be down with Reiki — but he was open because he wanted to heal. Quickly.

When we lose our health, pride soon follows. Sickness offers a clear chance to renew our focus on the body. That's what I love about this work: it heals me, too. I read somewhere that the only purpose we need in life is to be an open vessel. Healing energy dazzles because the Divine God/dess, etc uses us to heal another.

I used to get mad when my Mom responded to a compliment with the phrase, "It's not me; it's the Lord" — because I saw it as a negation of her role. I understand her meaning now, especially with a grateful client. It doesn't go to my head because it isn't me who heals.

It's difficult to describe what happens in a Reiki session because it's so intricate. It's as if I go beyond the human body and swim in waves of essence. Like touching water. When I start feeling that rhythm, I'm onto something. Craniosacral practitioners describe it in similar terms — working with the flow of the body.

Often it's a very gentle movement; no fireworks, lights or voices. It's an inner knowing of where to place my hands. Sometimes I feel heat, other times nothing. Despite what may randomly arise in my own self — doubt, worry, pain — the healing continues. What needs to get done, gets done. A client who is open and trusting only accelerates the process.

Healing starts with our beliefs about healing.

Being open heals me. I joked with my friend and said, "I've never touched a man for this long," and he laughingly replied, "Aw, we're not all bad." I patted his chest and said, "I know." Reiki requires me to be vulnerable and stretch in a way that's not always comfortable. Being that close is not easy — but I'm committed to my work and willing to go beyond self-imposed limitations.

His little son watched Godzilla in the other room and fragments of the movie drifted in. I normally don't care for any noise but was glad to let it go this time — because I realized that even Godzilla wanted a peaceful life. When he gave that well-known roar, it sounded lonely.

Then the fairy voices came floating out of the movie: "You humans need to learn from your mistakes and correct them." Even a scaly dragon wanted to be healed and go home. He just had a fiery way of showing it.

We often pray for a miracle when sickness or a broken heart stops us in our tracks. I used to think that answers came out of thin air; that God would reach down and fix it all up. I'd want the person who hurt me to make it better and grew furious when they didn't.

I see now the purpose of a healer: to be available so that when a wounded person seeks us out — not us finding them — we guide them back to a recognition of wholeness. In doing so, we heal ourselves.

We heal the Earth.

And we heal the generations to come.

To birth, to flame.

To live, to heal.

To love, to dream.

To see, to speak.

Yes.

It's the only thing that matters.

TO LIVE, TO HEAL
{VIGNETTES OF EARTH}

MY LEFT SHOULDER (2010)

"That's 20 years of women right there," I said to my massage therapist as she dug out another seized muscle.

"More like high school. Feels old. Dark brown."

"That's J," I said. "Ninth grade." Oddly, all of my great loves start with J.

She kept chasing down the most elusive tensions but couldn't get them in an hour. My pain is very clever. It stays one step ahead — and isn't going without a fight.

My left shoulder is where I house all of my women. Mothers. Former lovers. Unfulfilled desire. Disappointment. Anger. Battles I didn't win. Betrayals. Devastating break-ups.

My shoulder has been demanding release of this pain in her fourth decade. Notice I didn't say *crying*. She's not that kind of shoulder.

By nature, my left shoulder is the one who carries the shield over my heart. The one who curls forward in defense if anyone approaches without a welcome. She is the fierce, unrelenting feminine. Amazon. Warrior. The one who will fight to the death.

But she's tired. Very, very tired.

This shoulder is the same one stabbed clean through during a previous war / barfight / joust. She carries what looks like a bruised scar with the point of exit right next to the blade. When I suffer a fresh sting, that point feels like the blazing letter of a branding iron.

Our bodies carry the stories of our lives. She is the elephant of memories — and will faithfully lumber along with those burdens until the day we drop this form. That's how loyal she is to us.

Except our bodies naturally want to be well.

I adore my body and am faithful in return by releasing what nails my muscles to a stamped timeline. What kind of healer would I be if I didn't?

This map is easy to follow. What we need to do is listen and be aware of our pain rather than ignore it — then take conscious action to heal what keeps us in bondage.

Action such as: massage, Reiki, craniosacral and other energy modalities, talk therapy, writing, walking, praying, confronting the one who hurt. Naming the lovers, one by one.

It's a very personal path, this one of healing. It only works when you approach your body with patience, love and lots of integrity. Our bodies are primed for healing. They dig a harmonious existence. They want to be free.

She will continue to ask — or demand, if it's my left shoulder — to pardon her from the prison of memory.

We're not meant to live in pain. Our bodies are not meant to be the whipping posts of regret. They house the Spirit, the Divine temple. They are the walking, fleshy manifestation of the All-That-Is — my new favorite word for God — which makes me even more eager to find out what life is like with a happy shoulder.

MEDITATIONS ON GRAY HAIR

With this new decade comes gray hair. Not the strands of my 30s. If only. I'm talking swaths around my right ear and lines of white through the front and back. My NYC stylist was correct in her warning not to pluck. I scoffed then and knew my hair would always be raven black. Blue-black. The hair everyone commented on at the salon. Thick and dark with a silky coarseness thanks to my Mexican ancestors.

Man, am I vain about my hair. You'd never know it since I'm a wash-and-go kind of girl . . . but I am vain. Happily vain, proudly vain – until standing before the mirror of truth. Then I slowly lean forward and say, What. in. the. hell. is. this? I'll run my hands through cascading silver and flip it to see that the right has more than the left, thanks to all that plucking. The front streaks were long in coming but are now here to welcome the second half.

I joke about making my gray hair part of my spiritual practice but it's actually true. It's time to dig deep and figure out what's been irksome about this change. I don't wear makeup. Never dyed or permed. My style is easy, thanks to living in Vermont. My diet is clean and organic. Body love and Goddess energy rocks. So, what gives?

My hair is my identity. When a friend annoyingly called me a brunette, I snapped, "My hair is black." It's what made me beautiful when I felt so ugly with thick glasses and broken teeth. It's what kept me connected to a mysterious genealogical line. It covered me in black.

A friend tapped me on the arm the other day and said, "Hey, you were in my vision this morning!" This is common Vermont vernacular.

She continued. "You were walking toward me but you were an Inuit, about 25, in an earlier lifetime. You were strong and stared straight ahead. When I called your name, you walked past and said, "I've kept my black hair in this lifetime so that you can recognize me."

That image is slowly changing and it unsettles me, as if dropping midway into another experience. It's being in a body that shifts before my eyes. It's embracing womanhood.

However, I can't help but think, who will I be with gray hair? How will people recognize me? Will they see me as old? Me, old??

It's hard pinpointing this trigger. Is this why Buddhists shave their head? It's not a fear of death; I welcome that mystery. Perhaps it's losing what I have seen as beautiful, this own self-recognition in physical form. Color and history. It's something to do with family.

On the subway in Mexico City, I finally saw people who looked like me — thick, dark hair, indigenous features and olive skin. They didn't ask me the perpetual question: What are you? Where are you from? I saw a mirror of my own self and finally felt recognized. Perhaps going "white" makes me reluctant to lose this slim connection.

So, I'll sit with the unease and encourage my melanin to manifest more black pigment. Nothing is impossible when I refuse to accept widely-held notions on aging.

Let's face it: women with well-kept silver hair are gorgeous. Classy. I love seeing a streak of gray in the front . . . on another woman's head. Fortunately, it seems that gray is becoming the new black.

I still prefer black.

HOW TO BE AGELESS

- Never say you're old. Ever.

- Moisturize. Often.

- You may be wiser, so act it by listening.

- Make *thank you* your constant mantra.

- Tip lavishly.

- Notice the homeless. They are you. Us.

- Forgive your greatest sin.

- Take long drives down familiar roads. See something new. Stop. Appreciate.

- Own a room without saying a word. There's nothing more arresting than a powerful woman.

- Be at peace with your silvers.

- Realize that life is long. Eternal.

- Avoid the news. It's mostly lies.

- Bless the world rather than curse it.

- Comfort your deepest disappointment.

- Find outlets for your beautiful, creative soul.

- Turn off the T.V. Shut down the computer. Breathe.

- Use the good plates and cloth napkins while eating wings. Buy the better wine.

- Appreciate those in the service industry. They make your life easier.

- Honor and respect your precious body. She is your most loyal friend.

- Explore past lives but live in the now.

- Heal yourself. Healing starts with your beliefs about healing.

- Notice what your mouth craves and see if it matches what your immune system needs.

- Let people love you.

- Admit that you enjoy talking to yourself.

- There are times of sex and times of celibacy. That's life. Embrace the power of both.

- Laugh at your (<u>insert religion</u>) guilt.

- Make love to Nature.

- Know that a few thrive on deception — but most reach for truth.

- Accept where you are, while saying *yes* to life.

- Release the one who got away.

- Listen to your pets. They offer you the opportunity to be a better person.

- Rest your eyes. Often.

- Love and worship your feet daily.

- Buy good bras. Wear them less.

- Before falling asleep, tell each part of your body to relax.

- Send love to your lymph nodes. They are fearless warriors who need regular rest.

- Your parents' disappointments are not your responsibility. Let go of the burden.

- Spend as much time improving your self as you do your partner's. One life is plenty.

- Make friends with your anger. Ask her what she needs. Give her comfort.

- Stop calling countries *3rd world*. We're all human and live on the same planet.

- Root out the inner sexist, homophobic tyrant. Then there's one less in the world.

- Strive for impeccability.

- Know that you know nothing.

- Feel pain. Don't run from it. It wants your attention for a reason.

- Make room for the Crone.

- The Goddess resides in all shapes and colors. You're no better with a tight ass than a flabby one.

- Take long baths. Light candles. Slow down. Breathe. Prana is life.

- Garlic is your friend. So is ginger. So is your bed.

- Buy nothing less than 600 thread count.

- Change your story. Be open to revision.

- Welcome the lessons of regret.

- Learn to say no. Then learn the art of delegation.

- You're not meant to heal the world. Heal yourself.

- Often doctors are wrong. Remember this when you are terrified.

- Notice the inherent gorgeousness of a sliced vegetable. Kiss it.

- Laugh at life's ridiculousness. Don't take yourself so seriously.

- Be open to bartering. It could be a divinely appointed moment. Don't pass it up because they can't pay your rate.

- Wear precious gemstones. Beauty doesn't want to be in a box.

- As much as you ask for Divine help, give it in return. In spades.

- Honor your dignity. There's no one like you.

- Don't believe the hype about aging. You're ageless.

REST EASY, HEALER

Often clients ask: *How do I become more intuitive? How can I stay connected?*

It's very easy.

Rest.

There's nothing more important for a healer.

Rest that visionary mind.

Rest that loving heart that always wants to help.

Rest from frantic. Rest from the need to save.

Rest from the questions that whirl around that seeking soul.

We are taught a false value in working hard, as if toiling to the point of exhaustion is something to be honored. Release yourself from that back-breaking illusion.

You can't save anyone, healer. You can't rescue anyone.

The true value is in renewal.

Want to be successful in this work? Honor yourself enough to rest. Give yourself permission to sleep in. Play. Indulge. That means: napping, sitting still, doing nothing, daydreaming, sipping hot tea, a glorious massage. It means letting someone love you. Listen to you. Rest with you.

Challenging times are ahead and your full capacities will be called upon. It's extremely important to soothe yourself. To cherish that sensitive, dignified heart.

Rest. It's one the easiest ways to stay connected.

POWER IN THE BLOOD

It's been said that women are at the heights of power during their period/cycle/moon.

Surely this is the greatest koan from the Universe. Bloating, grumpiness, anxiety, pain, exhaustion, cravings and messy blood translate to *power?*

Religious leaders and shamans must have known this when they banned bleeding women from ceremonies. I was offended until I realized why: they feared the power of menstruating women. Our blood affected the surrounding energies . . . so, get out.

I once sang in church, *the power in the blood, the power in the blood of the Lamb.* The suffering blood of Christ that heals and restores.

Eckhart Tolle stated that we females experience the collective generational pain during our moons. He encouraged us to sit with the suffering and transform it.

Typical man, I thought. *He'd change his tune after one period.*

As I sat in my monthly discomfort, I asked the Thoth deck: "What is the source of our power during our periods?"

Lo and behold . . . 3 of Swords. Pain. Heartbreak. Ultimate liberation.

I laughed.

The 3 of Swords represents pain that can't be Adviled into submission. The despair that resists chatter. It's surrender disguised as defeat. It's the no-bullshit purifying bath of pain. Connecting to the lost dreams of my mother. Sensing my daughters who will never be born. It's striking out at spirits who approach with ominous intent and seeing them pass like water through my hand.

It's being honest and admitting, *it really can suck to be a woman* because we bear the greater burden of pain on this planet.

My life passes with each period and allows a deeper understanding of the red tent. This is why women bleed into the earth and how the earth — our Mother — receives our blood.

Our pain.

Being a typical Gemini, I turned over a clarifying card because one is never enough. What appeared?

Ace of Cups. The deepest of water. Overflowing love. Peace. The feminine principle that soothes and restores.

When we acknowledge and heal the pain in our own blood, it not only frees us but the women to come.

This is true power. The power in the blood.

IN THE CLASSROOM OF THE CRONE

Neck muscles like ropes.

Red hair flowing down well past her shoulders.

Body tight, with the carriage of a dancer.

I mentioned that I was uncomfortable doing a headstand since I was on my period.

"Oh, I'm so old, I wouldn't know anything about that," she joked.

Old? I thought. She couldn't have been past 55. Her enviable body swooped around our yoga class while her brain believed that she was old.

Said obviously in jest but I could tell by the way she emphasized *old* that she meant it. Felt it. As if menopause wiped out every refrain of youth.

Her statement added one more to the plethora I've heard from women in their 50s on up. Since I am less than a decade from that decade, I pay attention.

What these women don't realize is that I listen.

They are the matriarchy for me.

They are teaching me how to embrace change, embrace the aging body, embrace what is left of this particular experience before moving onto the next.

They are my teachers. They are the Crone.

Unfortunately, very few have been taught in the ways of the Wise Woman. There is a huge disconnect in society to this prescient being — and we need her more than ever.

I'm not blaming the media. The media reflects what we want to see and hear.

I'm not judging women. Everyone's life is their own with which to play.

However, what I'd like women to know — and I greatly admire connected, older women — is that I am in their classroom right now. I was raised to believe that women were submissive to men and act as a dry erase board. Seen, not heard. The audience, not the teacher. The mother/wife with no other aspirations who slowly fades away.

I've had to re-learn everything, while never believing it in the first place.

Now that I approach the last half of my life — which I happily embrace — I am calling the Wise Women. The ones who welcome my emerging Crone. My grandmothers and mother are gone. I need my teachers.

I'm not age-obsessed. I'm wisdom-obsessed. Why do you think I returned? Feminine energies are deeply transforming the Earth. Who better to represent her than the women who possess the magical mystery of the Crone?

This isn't about death. It's never simply about death. The Crone is the woman with the ability to see beyond "this mortal coil" — and truly, she's faced death again and again. She is one who can play in the vortex of eternity. She is the ultimate healer because she has been both Maiden and Mother, whether or not she has had children in this lifetime.

"You're in the most powerful period of your life right now," I said.

"Really? How?"

"You've moved beyond the time of your blood — which is why men separated women because they feared and respected its power — and now you have all of the wisdom of the Maiden and the Mother to use. You've got it all. Very magical."

These statements can easily end up on the junkheap of pretty sounding words. Magic and power and baking bread take practice as much as belief. If we've grown up with connected women, then our union with the Crone will be much easier. If we see her as a bitter old thing, invisible to society, then it will surely be an uphill battle as we enter the mystery.

Re-think the fairy tales. Women are the change. Women are the example. And good lord, how can a powerful woman *ever* be invisible? We are as invisible as invisible does.

Quite often, this feeling of invisibility is in direct relation to being noticed by men. The ever-present "male gaze" which has turned elsewhere.

There are others who notice you. Namely, younger women.

Believe in your wise soul. Women like me — who look up to you — are listening.

DEATH OF A SHAMAN

I used to think that a shaman's death required total submission to the teachings of elders. It included mental flogging and physical discomfort such as a night in the freezing woods or fasting for a week. It required leaving the world to emerge reborn. It meant $6,000 to study with a white guy named Craig/Skyhawk in Sedona. Naturally, the teachers were male.

All this? Illusion. The shaman's death is quite simple once we see that the real deal checks in every day. The modern concepts of Death need to exit stage right to understand this. Lack of direction and feeling disconnected from love only accentuate Death's final entrance.

The shaman's death is certainly a strip-down: to be utterly, completely naked in front of your own life. Exposed to the higher realities. To see life for what it is . . . and sorely isn't. To notice gray hairs and know that the world continues despite them. It's not a fear of physical death, per se; it's the canvas of now, a cavernous space where all disappear.

When Bat fell out of the *Animal Medicine Cards* and also swung very much alive under my chair two autumns ago, something was afoot — and I was afraid. The warning of rebirth was immediately translated as death. *Who's gonna die?*

Rebirth is a nice concept, except when faced full on. My ego rises like a vengeful ghost wielding a pretty heavy sword once change comes to my door.

I am always nervous when facing the unknown. *What's next? Who will I become?* Same goes for the graying of my black hair. That new picture is uncomfortable. Unacceptable.

It's ego. Vanity. Change I can't control.

Who I am when I disappear?

Hair is the shiny surface. Let's talk the real-deal shit. When money dries up. When a lover walks out. When a parent dies. When I wake with sore limbs. The years of stress and trust and not knowing. It's as if my wiser self says, "Okay, you've learned and expanded so much. Let's see how you *really* do with opening your heart," and then proceeds to place one uncomfortable situation after another in front of my nose.

Welcome to this shaman's death.

Ah, yes. My heart. It really hasn't been about money or gigs. It isn't about living in the perfect apartment or writing a bestseller. It isn't about magical sex. It's about my heart.

When friends once said things like, "You are loved. Love protects you," I instantly dismissed them. Those airy-fairy statements were too close to the evangelical messages that were laced with hypocrisy. It didn't bring the true meaning of love any closer.

Over the years, I've had to create my own mantra:

I will always love, protect and appreciate my body.

I will be devoted to myself which naturally leads to respect for another.

That's as near as I get.

This mash-up of shamanic death and financial strain has made reliance on others my thorn. It's never been my forte because it reflects badly on this Amazonian nature.

Women get it done. Right? Except this woman is *tired*.

I chose to winter in Florida while acutely aware that help was required: from parents, best friend and Vermont family. Asking for money was the last thing I wanted. Living with my friend in her studio was uncomfortable. Finding a place in Vermont was intensely stressful.

Yet there was work to do. Time to welcome vulnerability. Why? To open my heart. To develop even more empathy. To understand in hindsight that it was all preparation for my mom's passing. Little Bat was my teacher in showing me how to step out in faith and embrace this friend called Death.

RELEASE

January seems to be the month of death around these parts.

No surprise there. If I were in a creaky body, the perfect time for release would be when the world is most inhospitable to my bones.

The latest was a friend of the family, almost a year to the day of my mom's death. She was our former pastor's wife who was from the stoic generation. Very sharp mind. Kind soul. As she was dying, she requested to speak with me.

"She's the tall one, right?" she asked my Dad as he called my phone.

Her voice was still strong after 93 years of roaming this place.

I told her how much I admired her strength.

I don't know about that. What do you mean? she said.

You have such a strong spirit, I replied. *I can feel it.*

Again, she demurred.

Well, maybe our strength is in our doubts, I finally said.

To that, she agreed.

Four bowls of ice cream later, she passed on from this world.

January is the season of release. The hard month that hides the softness of transition.

On 11/11 last year, I dreamed of my Mom. She didn't look like herself but rocked more of a young Joyce Carol Oates persona.

I said, *Mom! How are you doing? How's heaven?*

It's not what people read about in books, she said. *But it's very beautiful.*

That got me excited, as if I'd already visited and couldn't wait to get back. We then switched to communicating telepathically and she gestured to show that heaven was right next to me, not above. Literally a footstep away in another dimension.

Death is easy, she said. *You close your eyes and drop the form. Humans make it so difficult.*

Perhaps that's the nature of release. We think we know how — then screw it up by resisting. These squishy forms get us all tied up in this thing called time. When it comes to an old lover or an aging body, time frames really don't work.

Get over it. Let go. Release. The words we say to offer balm.

It may take a month or a life to make peace with dropping the form.

To release those sweet dreams, unfulfilled.

Release the fantasy of a life not lived with another.

Release the idea that youth is the only blessing.

Release the carefully crafted lives that swoop across the field in a snowy waltz.

Maybe strength does indeed live within our doubts.

THE ONLY ANSWER

Many self-righteous, frightened people surrounded me in the evangelical community of my youth. This naturally planted a distrust of anything that was considered *worldly*. Jesus was right when he advised to be *in the world but not of the world*, so I hung out exclusively with born-agains and was schooled at Christian institutions from 7th grade through college.

Following a path that was clearly not carved for my steps only ended in frustration. It didn't make me any less gay. It didn't take away my ingrained curiosity about the world. It only helped foster a pattern of suspicion that persists to this day. The black and white kind. Not about skin color — but overall human behavior.

This is right. You are wrong. This is the truth.

Suspicion towards: the ranting, humorless vegans. The homophobic, sign-wielding churchgoers. Sexist, selfish men who act from a sense of pure entitlement. Women who so easily lay down their power. Bitter elderly who would as soon run your ass over. Ungrateful clients who don't like what they hear. The scornful glances cast at my profession. The general state of viciousness that lies beneath the veneer of civility.

All of this could make me a bitter misanthrope. Believe me, I still can't rub shoulders too long in this world. Plenty of renewal time is needed to remember again why I love it so.

This beautiful, terrible world full of gentle flowers that bloom anywhere once given enough sunlight and water. The animals who assist and nurture. The courage of those in the midst of healing their deepest pain.

Self-righteousness is the easiest way to stay disconnected from wholeness. Anyone can practice it, including healers who claim that this dimension is too heavy for their spirit.

It reminds me of that old joke where a Muslim boy and his father play catch in heaven. The boy points and says, "What's the huge wall over there?"

The dad replies, "That's where the Christians live. They think heaven is only for them."

Self-righteousness only cements very high walls around our loneliness. It's says, *I'm better because I think/do/act in a "more right" way. I know the truth. You don't. When I'm done with this sucky life, there's a reward just for me. Sorry, you don't get any. Just me.*

If only it were that easy. If only it worked in such a simple manner.

Slice the baby in two. Simple and clean.

Solomon got this one right. Don't get me started on his 1,000 women, though.

Bring it back to the self so frightened of shining. The self that hides behind the clothing of a queen, tyrant or beggar holding a sign that says: *Only me. Not you.*

What if this separation is merely a hungry illusion that we keep feeding?

Exclusivity is the oldest marketing trick in the book. Please follow the blinking neon arrow back to your junior high school gym class.

It all comes back to the ill-fitting clothes, the broken teeth, the crooked glasses.

It all comes back to the screaming father, the cowering mother, the lonely days.

It all comes back to claiming our place in this world without taking from another.

To feel safe enough in knowing that this experience can be a generous one.

If we let it be. Let it be so.

The only answer to our self-righteousness is laughter.

MY ANGELS PREFER HARLEYS

"I have Mafioso angels. No, seriously," I said and swooped my hands in a wide arc before falling back in my bamboo chair.

"I believe you, Raven," my client laughed. "You look like a giant angel. In fact, you *are* an angel to me."

I've always felt protected. Massively, intensely protected. Do I know the names of my guides? Nope – but they are the biggest, most bad-assed angels you'd ever NOT want to meet. They circle me like Secret Service agents but rarely intervene unless it is to save my life.

They were my essential chip in pre-birth negotiations. Before squeezing into a womb, I said, "Okay. I'll return to Earth under somewhat arduous conditions: single Catholic mom, given up at birth, foster care, won't know my birthparents, adopted into a fundamentalist family with a raging father. No problem — but I request the best angelic protection in return."

They agreed and lined up the burly ones. If these guys could slap on leathers, they would. Surprisingly, they're all male. They guard my four corners while extending an arms-length aura. They wield amazing power but respect and admire my strength. I've walked down South Bronx streets that would make grown men quiver. No one has ever touched me.

I especially feel the one to my left, the guardian of my heart. He reminds me of a beautiful black man with arms the size of tree trunks who works as a bouncer at the most exclusive club in L.A. He's got that "stand back" attitude. No one messes with him.

My angels point like stars and I feel them like foundation.

I even dreamed of them years ago: a heavenly host of angels all suited up in leathers and flying west across the sky.

They may have wings, but my angels prefer Harleys.

THE GUARDIAN OF THE GEMSTONES

"He's the Guardian of the gemstones," she said, pointing to the wall. Stones clicked in her palm like marbles.

Her phrase lit up my heart, as evidenced from the immediate goosebumps on my arm, up through my neck and around my scalp.

The Guardian of the gemstones. I repeated the statement at least twice and it made complete sense. Flowers and animals had their guardians but I never really contemplated that these ancient beings did, as well.

She nodded. "I can show you his picture. It's amazing. A woman did an intuitive drawing for me in a session. That's where it belongs," she said, pointing up again to a place on the mantle above the baskets of stones at Pyramid.

Be in this work long enough and these conversations are commonplace. The weirder, the better. Messengers in my past were usually lumped as schizophrenic and I turned away from anything that veered from "normal" into bizarre concepts such as plant spirits, UFOs, ghosts and the like. None of that crazy shit for me.

Not anymore. I wouldn't be a very good healer if my mind wasn't open to what is considered odd or out of the ordinary. It simply took time for my palate to grow used to the subjects. Now I say: *more, please.*

It also takes a certain amount of trust to speak on topics which give life to our hearts. This particular woman couldn't get enough of stones. They spoke to her in a language that she subsisted on daily.

However, her intuition guided and warned her when to speak. The old throwing-your-pearls-to-swine thing.

I know this sounds crazy . . . I can't believe I'm about to say this . . . I almost can't tell you; it sounds so weird . . . you won't believe me. My clients utter these statements with either a look of pure fear or bemused embarrassment.

"Uh, look where you are," I say and start to laugh, fanning my arms out like a showgirl.

Too crazy? Take a closer view. Here I am: perched on the edge of a slatted bamboo chair that cracks at the most inopportune moments in a sunny meditation room filled with Himalayan salt crystals while hovering over three Tarot decks and a table full of gemstones, waiting to hear tales of an extraordinary life. Yours.

You've come to the right place. It's never too weird.

COMFREY COMFORT

Why is it that children so easily believe in fairies? Spirits? Angels?

Why is it that adults often have to go through a period of re-belief?

I did a session for a woman exiting a long period of heartbreak and disappointment in the promise of life. I did see brightness and real possibilities soon to enter but wasn't sure if she believed me. Yet she had enough hope or politeness to listen.

We then strolled around her lovely farm while the geese waddled and clacked nearby. The flowers were in full bloom with the flirty peonies as sassy as ever. My client pointed to a swath of vegetation and said, "Comfrey. It's taking over the garden. I've got to cut it back."

If you know me, you know I work in symbols. A cigar is never just a cigar.

It took me a minute and then I laughed. Comfrey. Of course.

"Well, you did ask for comfort and protection."

"What do you mean?" she asked.

"Comfrey heals bruises and reduces swelling. It's the heart healer. It knits bones together. Maybe that's why it's wrapping around your house?"

She stopped. Considered. Then smiled and shook her head.

"I never thought about it that way."

I love how the great Mother provides us with everything we need, if only we can see it.

It's easy to get angry when disasters arrive. We can be quick blame what we consider the erratic behavior of Nature and careless humans who trample over our hearts.

How often then do we say *thank you* to the plants who stand ready to heal?

SOMEDAY THE PAST WILL HEAL

Someone clear across the continent found my site through this keyword search: *someday the past will heal.*

Does the past ever heal?

I'm not sure if it does. That may surprise you, considering my work. Heal often means: "Go away", "Forget it", "That was years ago!", "Let's not talk about it", "Water under the bridge", "Haven't you been grieving long enough?"

Our wounds have to go somewhere, so the body will absorb them while the mind creates and repeats a story to keep them alive. Basic survival instincts.

Once we begin to wake up and outgrow the stories, we arrive at a place of compassion. It's taken me decades to make friends with my anger, to really listen to what she's trying to say. It's very uncomfortable acknowledging this. Aren't I a woman of constant equilibrium?

Coming to terms doesn't negate what went down in the past to cause the anger — but when I see myself as an active participant in my own life, it makes more sense.

What went down got me here.

Here, right now — human, happy and whole.

Let's step back. What if I set this up before birth? What if I asked for an challenging first half? What if I've known the significant players on my stage for many lifetimes and we agreed to continue working out our stuff in this one?

I have an image of us meeting up after we leave our bodies behind. We'll laugh and say, "Man, you were such a good actor. You played that role to the hilt. You were SUCH a bastard!" Then we'll think it's just incredibly hilarious.

Healing is about transmutation. Snake in the *Animal Medicine Cards* represents the ability to transform any poison into balm. We've always been whole and always will be. The past doesn't divide the circle. It may be tempting to forget our humanity but Snake doesn't lose its being after shedding the outer shell.

This idea of the *wounded healer* is outgrown. I'd rather be a whole healer smoothing my sharp edges with peace and asking Wisdom to teach the purpose of such irritating pain.

Perhaps even the term *past* is less than beneficial. The energy directed at our most intense stories refills the mental IV drip. As I listen to Peter Gabriel's *Us*, I am immediately transported to a Toyota stuffed with boxes, driving West and crying over my girlfriend. The experience rises; my heart is broken again as my relationship is sung away through the lyrics.

Should my emotions be squelched with a condescending tone? "Raven, that was 20 years ago!" Sure, but they'll swing right back again to be healed. There is no dismissing pain.

Instead, I can offer compassion to the me who was so hurt then — but I'm able to say goodbye. If and when she returns, we'll continue. The more I acutely listen, the less these conversations are needed.

The end? It's ultimately about release. Freedom. And forgiveness.

Ah, forgiveness. The word most bandied about during my youth. It's so key. I once hated the concept because it made me feel weak, like I was allowing *them* to hurt me and damned if that was going to happen. But oh, forgiveness. It's the deepest way of making friends with myself for being exactly who I am.

So tricky, this self-loving minefield. So hard to navigate without a sword. So not my style. Yet in my 4th decade, the only thing that will work.

TIPS FROM A SUCKY MEDITATOR

I'm a sucky meditator. Always have been.

I also failed at being a successful prayer warrior. I either chanted the popular evangelical mantra, "I just ask, Lord" (with the *yes, Jesus* chorus in the background) or practiced a grasping neediness in private to a disapproving male god.

I tried my best. *Responsible* was my middle name.

One way or the other, it didn't feel like communion.

Good thing that life is long and we have time to navel gaze. God/dess is often found beneath the lint.

When I hear the word meditation, it translates to a rule: sit, be still for *x* amount of minutes and watch thoughts go by. Try not to squirm. Be a good little Buddha.

Bleh. As hard as a church pew.

Now contemplation? Dig. Practice daily contemplation? Yes. To be in a place of thoughtful thinking? Always.

Stillness — is — necessary, as my active Gemini mind can drive me nuts. However, I don't call it meditation. I call it: sit down and actively encourage limbs to relax. Don't think — but if I do, whatever — then bring it back to relaxation. No figuring it out, no chastising, no need to feel particularly spiritual. *Chill*. That's enough.

You don't have to meditate to be spiritual. You don't have to pray to touch God. In fact, we'd be better off throwing out the names altogether.

Much of this spiritual stuff is like standing on the edge of a swamp. So ego based. *Oh, I can hold this pose longer. Sit straighter. Pray more beautifully. Get sharper psychic hits. Go to church 7 times a week. Proudly hold a title. Draw huge, adoring crowds for the sake of drawing huge, adoring crowds. Stay in an ashram and brag about mastering austerity. Humbly, of course. I'm so spiritual. Isn't it sexy?*

When you grow up in the evangelical world like I did, talk about being schooled. I observed and practiced so much hypocrisy wrapped in spiritual talk. There was a desperate need for attention in the guise of searching for God, as if we lost her long ago in a dusty closet.

Meditation and prayer feel hard because I never feel spiritual enough. My humanity is right on the tender surface. I'm no saint (and I have a list of ex-girlfriends who would happily agree.) I'm very human. That's the thing. I *like* being human. I like feeling my muscles contract and expand. I like — yes — even the messiness of relationships and a crappy, burned pizza. There's a sweetness to it all.

Forgiveness is easier now when I fall short of the lofty goals set under the priority list of A PERFECT LIFE. As I came into this world, I will slip right out, still praising the beauty of this place. I'll praise my body who has walked so faithfully with me, protecting my sweet heart. I will have seen it all: the faintest flower, the desperate aspirations, the oneness of our separation.

The way I get God now is in direct proportion to the amount of love I extend. How comfortable I am in my skin. How easy it is to be generous in this particular lifetime. How involved I am with ordinary beauty. To know that I am as great as anyone else.

Instead of meditation, I'll rest my bones for awhile over a steaming cup of tea. I'll look over to see God/dess relaxing in the chair across from me, smiling and nodding.

Now *that* I can do.

OUR SMALL PLACES

I often take Vermont's healing powers for granted. This summer has been one of the most beautiful: languid sunsets, layer upon layer of green mountains, fecund air and exploding gardens. Everything is happy.

My Dad recently visited and I am usually filled with anxiety. I'm 41. I know my strength. It's taken years to heal from childhood wounds. Yet when Dad shows up, it's like I haven't moved an inch. At least that's the illusion, the imprint, my mind holds. I feel small.

Until Dad actually arrives and I see how frail he's become. The passing of my Mom after nearly 50 years of marriage has left him adrift. He gets lost on routes they traveled a million times. He loathes being alone. He's forgetful but still retains the life force of a Gemini. He's less eager to nitpick and disapprove. In fact, I think he's learning how to listen.

It would be easy to say that I feel sorry for his pain but it's more than that. It's a tenderness towards life: how short our lives are within eternity. How we hurt each other from all our small places. How life changes in a moment so that it is unrecognizable from the last.

I jumped in my seat when a raven screamed from the trees as Dad walked to my car. After I left, another raven swooped low across my sunroof and extended her glossy winged undercoat, as if wrapping her "arm" around my car. I raised my hand in a wave to thank her.

When I drove back home through the hills, the air was fragrant and the roads empty. I still felt that little raging girl wandering around inside who had so much to say.

I said, *I hear you. I'll always listen. You don't have to carry that heavy load anymore. Let me take it on. I just want you to be happy and free and play.*

She smiled at me, then ran off.

THE PATH OF LEAST RESISTANCE

As I had brunch with a friend, her daughter suddenly rushed into the Moon Dog and ran to our table with bike helmet askew. She's all of 8 and I call her my "little warrior". She loves to launch herself at me — poking, prodding and cracking jokes about my butt. This time, she immediately complained about a boy and I said, "Did he bother you? 'Cause I'll kill him. No, I will." She smirked, looking quite pleased. Her mom laughed and said, "I wouldn't want to see you with your mean face on. I'd run, for sure." This from a strong woman herself but I knew that even as we giggled, she'd probably run.

My mean face isn't pretty. It was often used to keep classrooms under control and I waded through the wreckage of personal relationships as a result. Where did I first learn to fight? Two older brothers and a domineering father. I reluctantly bought the line that women couldn't speak in church — or anywhere — with authority. I wore thick glasses, was smart, creative and carried an old soul. I played well at sports. I didn't flirt with boys. I fought with words, not fists but often received the latter. Sometimes I stayed silent and hated myself for it.

And man, have I fought in life. Maybe it's my Aquarius moon and Scorpio ascendant, signs that fight every injustice on the planet. Look at me the wrong way? Fight. Say the wrong thing? Fight. Bother a friend? Fight. Criticize? Fight. On and on.

Though I prefer to stray from the trail when I walk through the woods, I still seek the path of least resistance. The deer paths. The line of the river. Streams cutting downhill. Sure, I could plow past the thin pine branches and scurry over rocks — but why? The trees are just as beautiful on the easier path.

It took many trials and tribulations to understand that life isn't any less meaningful if it isn't hard. It's okay to want an easy life.

Christianity demands that we gird ourselves against Satan or the sinful flesh. To be distrustful of outsiders — i.e., to not be "unevenly yoked". The ever-present war was there to fight on a daily basis, so fight I did.

It was a religion of perpetual exhaustion.

I was often called stubborn and rebellious despite living a responsible life. Even before fully embracing my power as a woman, I fought anyone who told me what to do or how to be. That mean face was created to not only say *fuck you* but also to give my warrior an outlet. If I couldn't speak, my face would damn well reveal my truth.

A tough exterior hid a soft heart. As a young adult, I let that sword go whenever needed. Screw love — though I always felt sorry and doubtful while picking through the detritus.

Years and wisdom certainly have a voice here. So does my sensitive spirit that thrives when balanced. It's about making friends with my anger and letting shit go. Seriously. I have to say, "Raven, let that shit go. It's not worth it."

The difference now? I do.

Working as a healer has opened my heart in ways unimaginable. It's shown that we all have broken pieces that continually cut us; ragged wounds we carry with such courage until resolution. Wholeness. It's necessary to learn how to live with our inner warrior to get there.

The urge to lash out still exists, but I also attempt to see both sides until peace comes. The scorched earth policy isn't so appealing anymore. I'm choosing to walk the path of peace. Allowing an easy, balanced flow.

I'm trying my best.

Rarely do I show my mean face now — but know she's there when I need her.

ISN'T IT CHRONIC?

I have spent most of my life worrying about things that never happened.
~Mark Twain

Eckhart Tolle's voice can lull me to sleep but his message — wow. Definitely opens up the possibility of the moment, which can be one of two things: big, fat stress or perfection.

Don't get me wrong. I am far from guru status. What I practice is staying in the moment, and it's kind of a bitch. However, if I can be still and focus — *I have everything I need right now* — then the stress of the next minute fades.

This thing called time can really trip us up to the core. So can the green stuff.

While strolling a gorgeous beach, I caught myself reciting monthly patterns of worry. *Rent, bills, rent, bills.* It's a nurtured addiction that provides the illusion of control. Worry can find me even on an exquisite Caribbean island and ruin everything.

Right then, I decided to allow vulnerability a place in the midst of financial distress. I didn't dwell on the worst but remembered times when money has come. I've always paid my bills and still eat organic. I live in a lovely home, drive a new car and have a flexible schedule.

Once the material dropped away, I saw that the basic foundation of my life is already in place: the freedom, innate strength, intelligence and hustle that brings constant opportunity. My bank account may not fully reflect it, but doesn't negate its truth.

Being a healer is having an unshakable faith in the goodness of life. It's showing up with courage. Like Chiron the wounded healer, the remembrance of suffering is always near — yet this moment brings perfection, the stillness found in the present. The only thing we have.

Time to set up permanent shop there.

RICHNESS

One friend has $700 worth of repairs on her car.

Another wonders how she'll pay the rent to keep her cafe open.

Another has stopped eating meat because she can't afford to buy it.

And another is blazing forward with her intuitive biz.

I'm all for Abraham-Hicks and the law of attraction. I love positive thinking — but not at the expense of acknowledging struggle.

Struggle is different from wallow. Struggle is empathy because yeah, I've been there. Time and time again. Saturn roams my chart this particular lifetime to teach me about money. Which means I've known wealth and long for it again.

It's time to re-think and re-tune these ideas of richness. I wouldn't be living in Vermont if my desire for success was on a strictly green basis. This is the state of healing, good vibes and gorgeous vistas. Not necessarily the land of fat cats and fatter wallets. But it's frustrating when I can't write a check to help friends out of a tough spot. Wouldn't that be great?

I want life to be easy. For them. For me. I've known plenty of rich people who struggle in their souls but that doesn't make it better for any of us.

Hey, I'm not a healer who's all *la-la* about abundance. Not having cash sucks.

Why have we chosen this green piece of paper to make the world go round? We're shaped from living in a place that requires money. It's pretty odd. I've made it a lifetime goal to be more like water, less like rock. To willingly receive support and make this ride smoother. That includes coinage.

Sure, there are ways of being frugal. Or ways of spending without a care. Or staying somewhere in the middle. It's that sense of *not enough* that haunts.

My needs are always met. Always. My bills are paid. It may be at the very last minute that cash arrives but it comes. Reminding myself of that fact is essential. It's like I suffer from perpetual monthly amnesia — or maybe have a slight addiction to worry.

The law of attraction can't work until I have compassion for where I am right now. That is a life well-lived with a perpetually low bank account — *low* being a relative word. That contrast is either a thorn in my side or the magical place where everything transforms. It's being at the crossroads of the 5 of Pentacles.

I dig the essence of money. I do love the ease it brings. Tipping well. Driving a BMW convertible. I love beauty — and money grants access to certain types. I love paying my bills and having plenty left over.

Saturn teaches me to stay in place long enough for the lesson. If I resist, he merely hangs around until enlightenment. I always have enough, while wanting more. The law of attraction may not resonate for you. So what? Find what works. Find what brings ease. Trade in your car. Refinance. Be grateful for every little thing. Every little thing. This works wonders for an anxious mind. You can still experience beauty while enhancing the picture. It doesn't take away from the fundamental form. Every painter knows that.

Every painter also knows when it's finished — or time to move onto another work.

Cars raced down the road this morning and I recalled what it was like to sip coffee and negotiate with angry drivers on a daily basis. Even if there was $500,000 or $50 in my bank account, I was still taking a walk: no hurry, no agenda. Admiring beautiful summer gardens and doing exactly as I pleased.

Unexpected bills may come. We may not have enough to pay the rent. Our savings may shrink in a volatile stock market. We may lose faith. We may get everything we ever wanted and fear the shoe drop. These moments of uncertainty shake us up. Why?

A caller phoned in for a reading on my show, "Tarot Talk". She was self-employed and kept asking, "When's the money coming?" I pulled the 3 of Swords which flew straight past her financial anxiety to an emotional wound. Her pain was trying to come out in the easiest way possible – through financial stress.

This isn't rocket science. Our wounds emerge where we are most anxious.

They're saying: *Heal me. Set me free.* It is like a perpetual cut on a child's wrist. She's tired of carrying it around. These wounds are not meant to kill us but they certainly do not wish to fester. They remain because we ignore them.

Our insecurities ask for transformation. They anticipate release.

Imagine ourselves as a medium for our wounds.

Calling them out.

Healing them.

Releasing them.

Knowing that this too, shall pass. It always does.

Or look up at the beautiful sky, take a deep breath and say:

"Gimme the money, honey!"

GOD OVER A ROAST BEEF SANDWICH

Lately, I've been wondering where God/dess has been hanging out in the Enchanted Forest. I need a little magic to jazz things up.

God came through as God is wont to do. Maybe God always does but I suffer from selective receptivity.

I'm on the phone with my Dad, coming out to him for the nth time and chipping away at his hardcore beliefs by stating: *this is who I've always been.* I tell him that it's awkward to never mention women I've loved, as if they didn't exist. He reiterates that being gay is sinful and a choice — *spoken like a true heterosexual,* I snap — but that he loves me.

His statement is probably all I'll get in this lifetime. Love . . . but. Stingy love.

Then this guy pulls up in a red truck and I immediately notice because he's black. Vermont is a very white state. White, white, white. So odd from my previous NYC life and the colors I sorely miss. He strolls into the Moon Dog wearing a white t-shirt, frayed jeans and boots. He's mid-60s and strong. Clean-shaven. Bald. A great match for my single friend, though I can already tell where his sights are set.

I say a quick hello as he slides himself onto the barstool two down and orders a roast beef. Within minutes, I nip his interest in the bud while continuing to chat. He's from South Carolina, married 5 times, a Reiki healer. So many stories, waiting to be told.

He's got me: I'm curious. What is it with these traveling magicians?

Then God comes sneaking up. Maybe it's how his watery-blue eyes unflinchingly concentrate on my face. Maybe it's the way he holds my words in complete and total acceptance when I share the freshly spoken conversation with Dad. We talk about how humans are walking manifestations of God and how difficult it is for me to love Divinity in the so-called followers of Christ. We share how all of us head towards God one way or another.

He tells about the time three teens circled him with ill intent and when he called out, "If what you're about to do brings you closer to God, do it," they scattered.

Somewhere in the midst of our conversation, the left side of my head begins to tingle. I pay closer attention. A certainty rises up: *This is God.*

Don't misunderstand: I see Ed. Ed is me and I am Ed. And not — but God is present. It happens. Not often enough, so I put my sensors on the highest frequency possible.

Then Ed grabs my hand for an impromptu reading. When he stares at my face to read its features, I calmly look back. I let myself be open — not something I normally do with any psychic. I listen. He sees the lost loves and hard-earned wisdom. He recognizes the sensuality in the space above my lips and sons waiting to be born. He speaks of my ever-thinking mind and how I must direct it, not turn it off. He mentions my fierce guardian angel.

I feel the energy in his worn hands and want him to hold mine a little longer. He smiles and says, "Okay. I'm late for my . . . wherever I have to go."

I hug him like a brother. I don't hand him my card or offer to meet up again. I do, however, say that I know God sent him — that S/he meant for us to connect.

He bows and strolls off.

Sometimes God shows up over a roast beef sandwich.

THE APPLE TREE IS MY OYSTER

An apple tree curves out from the hillside beyond my window. A few leaves cling to the finger-thin branches and shriveled apples quiver and shiver at the ends. Jays and chickadees muscle around the feeder. The tree, once a picture of fullness, stands bare in the icy snow. It felt as if summer was only yesterday; the unending richness of low-hanging apples. I used to lay beyond the branches as fruit landed right next to my chair. How tasty the ground must have been to the ants, bees and birds. A banquet.

The Goddess Tarot symbolizes the Ace of Pentacles as a gorgeous, rooted tree. By the time the hapless wanderer reaches the Five of Pentacles, life has shut its door. We are the outsiders; literally left in the cold.

What will get us beyond this crossroad? Having a generosity of spirit toward all things. Remembering the sweetness of life, even with a healthy disdain for winter.

Everything returns in time.

Otherwise, I might decide to chop down the apple tree if my eyes only saw a pathetically withered piece of wood. But promise runs beneath her bark, life-force in sap form. The deep roots sunk in a frozen marinade.

Ironically — if there's anything such as irony here — the branches sweep up and over the twisted trunk like the side ponytail of an '80s aerobics instructor, extending bony fingers above the pasture.

In which direction do they point? Everywhere.

NO SUCH THING

What happens when you are ready to leave?

When you hear the implicit *yes, it's time*.

Time for another town. Community. Imprint.

Time for souls yet to meet. Merge. Begin.

Time to walk on fresh, warm soil. To learn. To stretch.

When the wind carries you away from those you love, the circle grows.

It's gentle.

You know this.

Still, there's room for the voices. You know the ones.

The voices that say, *Don't go. Stay. Make it work. It's cozy. Why can't you make it work? It's so easy to stay.*

You know these voices. In fact, you've been to this débutante ball many times. The simple truth: it *has* worked. Exactly how you imagined it would.

Then, the end.

And you laugh, because you know there is no such thing.

TO SEE, TO SPEAK
{VIGNETTES OF AIR}

THIS MOUNTAIN YOU'VE BEEN CLIMBING:
SPEAK OF THAT. (1970)

In the beginning was the Mother.

Her voice: never quiet, never still.

This language you know. Born with it in your bones, speech, movement, breath. This catamount at the far edges, the highest point, lingers in the space that remains.

This mountain you've been climbing: speak of that. Knowledge beats like the startled updraft of a dove, whirring and whispering to you. The voices of women. The gospel never written. The solitude of silence. The complicity of millions.

What are words if not eternal? Somewhere in you this gospel has been written. Take out your pages, tear them up and write them again. The time is now when the mothers rise — not in vengeance but the patient anger of forbearance. The way of the mother: yes. A child rocking on her knee, blade against your throat. Wielding both.

Do you feel her image? Do you taste the gentle steel? The voices still skip in space like stones rippling the void.

Carry on, little atom.

Let us now speak of cruel fathers. The ones who tried to root out the rebel. Who beat submission in Christ's name. The ones who knighted you: survivor.

These are the ones who will leave this earth, raging the ventricular language which has failed them.

Do you understand? Those who adapt, survive.

The patriarchy is broken.

Inside every father is the Mother. In her silence, the world was born. When is she heard? In darkness. Find her yet again.

This is why you returned, you who taught the women. Your time is now, this time of peace. Healing rises. Eagerly, eagerly.

To be a woman of peace. To leave behind warrior ways. This is the time of restoration, as the ruins once called you home. You are here to lead the daughters.

In the beginning was the Mother.

GIVE IT AWAY NOW

Psychic Tip #1 *(yes, this is free)*: There are times you will make concerted efforts to book an appointment with a Tarot reader and *it will not work out*, no matter what you do. Don't push. Sit with the question. Let the plan already in motion unfold in its own time.

However, there are always those who keep pushing from fear or impatience, go to a random reader and promptly give away their power. Things inevitably fall apart after chasing whispers and soon they grow disillusioned. They may even call the psychic a *fraud*.

You know the old story about sheep + wool + eyes? Yeah. That one.

Too many give their power to "spiritual" people. They allow undue influence while their discernment stays on permanent vacation. I've had clients toss me theirs and I send it right back. Unfortunately, there are many unscrupulous folk who will gladly keep it.

Don't say I didn't warn you.

Psychics are not meant to give you a purpose or lay out a life plan for you.

This is called *giving away your power* when you ask for one.

We've been trained to find the all-consuming answer. You know, the one that fulfills every question, longing and problem in 30 minutes or less. We seek wisdom through parents, teachers and those behind the cards or the pulpit.

This may be surprising, but the people about whom I'm most skeptical are other psychics. Gurus. Pastors. The spiritual biz can be so tricky: full of ego, competition and fear. I'm passionate about stripping away the mystique while sharing its beautifully inherent magic.

Guess what? You don't ever really need a psychic.

That statement may put me out of business. So be it.

There's a scene in the lovely movie *La Vie En Rose* where Edith Piaf desperately visits a medium for weeks and the woman finally says, "Madame, what more can I tell you?"

Some like to be told what to do. Some want to endlessly re-live their sorrow. Some can't bear to courageously step out of their cozy pants.

Where's the growth in that?

True psychics are respectful guides. We're also human. We're not 100% accurate. We have our stuff. We're vulnerable and afraid, like you. The true psychics, the true healers, are all about freedom. A mutual empowerment. We don't take it personally if you decide that we are wise or full of shit. We're about expansion of mind and heart. We're about kindness and compassion. We deeply feel our humanness and carry a magic that is greater than this form — while knowing that our form is one of the greatest expressions of that power.

Many people find Shivaya Wellness through "psychic prediction 2012", as if 2012 is the answer. It's right now. The power we wield through our thoughts. Our words. How we carry ourselves in this world. What we allow to unfold. Whether our actions heal or destroy. The recognition that yes, all this affects our beloved planet long before 2012 — and long after.

Psychic Tip #2 *(still free)*: When we are careless with our power, we are certain to find opportunistic people who will happily manipulate it. Once we begin to honor our intuition — to know that every answer is within — then mutual partners will appear who are worthy of our time and $$$. We won't feel the need to give away our power in any form.

So bring the love and go within. Show me what you've got. Let that intuition shine.

I can feel your gorgeous magic all the way from here.

SECRETS FROM THE PSYCHIC WORLD

A massage therapist and I chatted at Pyramid the other day. He wondered if psychic abilities were real and inquired about my work. He also mentioned the Roma/gypsies who did readings in his native Poland. At times, one of the gypsies would point to a person in line and say, "No! Not you!" and dismiss them. No explanation. Just no, not you.

Though I was relatively comfortable speaking with him, I'm careful when using the word *psychic* because of the varying levels of emotional response. Such as: "You can predict the future?" or "I don't wanna know!" or "Oh, you see the future, Ms. Psychic? Let me prove you wrong," or conversely, "Oh, you were so right!"

It can really give a girl a complex.

When asked about the future, I'll answer like this: *Time* has no meaning. Age is an illusion we've created to understand the natural cycles of Earth and test our limits / lessness in this form. As for the future, I believe in free will and creating from the present.

Usually I say it fast and with confidence. It works wonders for the less-than-curious.

If we want to scratch this itch further, think of it this way: psychics "see" one future out of many, based on where you stand in life right now. If you decide to take the raisin out of your flakes, well, that will make a whole 'nuther breakfast. (Some people hate when you take out the raisin. They want it straight up with lots of milk and sugar — and if you change it by adding almond milk, then you've messed up the whole thing forever.)

Here's a HUGE secret from the world of psychics: there's nothing special about being psychic.

Did that knock your two-layered socks off or what?

Maybe you said, *Eh*, I already knew that.

Well, that makes you psychic. Congratulations!

Being psychic or an intuitive is like any other gift. Baking a perfect loaf. Planting a stunning garden. Fixing a complex engine. Giving a life-changing massage.

Everyone is unique. So, why is the term *psychic* exalted or vilified within seconds of uttering it?

It's been purposely made "evil" or "wow" to keep it separate from ordinary life. We are all given some type of intuitive ability. Former knowledge. The nudge that keeps us alive.

Why then the dissonance?

Many of us — particularly women — are taught to distrust our wisdom. To believe outside of ourselves in a god, a politician, TV character, our girlfriend or a psychic. So, we book a session and pay good money to have that wisdom reflected back to the extent that we can recognize it. There are plenty of frauds who take advantage. Stir up fear. Spray pesticides to the hilt. Bake a crappy loaf. Keep the oil cap off.

When we turn inward and really understand that we create the next step, every time, every day — we see the true value of healers; the ones who connect us to our own inner guide.

The psychic Edgar Cayce was a modern-day Cassandra who warned of greedy excess and war. Did that make him more special than, say, the person transcribing his notes? No. There's no difference. It doesn't matter what you call yourself. It's being devoted to your gift. That's where the healing resides.

There are varying types of intuitives who help in their own ways. Be grateful for that. For example, I don't assist police in locating missing children — but there are those blessed with the gift of being able to bear horrific visions that lead to closure.

Of course, there are psychics who think that their gift put them above everyone else.

A very, very dangerous trap.

I'd like to see psychic abilities taken down from their lofty perch and still be valued. I'd like people to be curious rather than frightened by their own knowledge that they, in turn, project onto genuine healers through religious aggression and downright condescension. People literally flinch or find me terribly interesting when I tell them my work. That's why I avoid the term *psychic* — for whatever reason, healer or intuitive is more palatable. Or writer/artist. Maybe that's why the Roma said, "No, not you!" because they didn't want to deal with the bullshit from an occasional heckler in the guise of a seeker.

At the end, my friend said, "So, psychics really aren't that special?"

"Nope," I replied. "We're just like everyone else." *

*Disclaimer: not to say my work isn't breathtakingly magical. It is.

157

STAR READERS

A few wacky New Age magazines occasionally cross my vision. I'll also confess to perusing *US Weekly* — as a sociological experiment. There's one woo-woo industry mag where the ads are filled with wild-eyed souls. Of course, the Tarot readers are the craziest. There's one who always makes me laugh which, upon reflection, is brilliant marketing.

She goes by her first name since surnames are *so* last lifetime. Let's call her Starella. A photo shows her in a huge cloak that seems to be made of the same material as the curtain behind her. That's not the arresting feature. In fact, it's rather blasé.

What draws me to the ad every time is a picture of the spirit/aura/soul of Starella floating out of the top of her head as if the 7th chakra threw open its windows to let out some steam. Her "spirit" face is much younger than the wig-wearing, heavily made up one that houses it and bears a passing resemblance to Joan Collins during the height of *Dynasty*.

Look, I'm trying not to judge but that's not my crew. Or are they? Starella and her floating spirit face are the unfortunate, universal billboard for Tarot readers. Include the strip-mall psychics with blinking red signs who fill out the package. I have a friend who always jokes, "Hey, where's your red lipstick?" and I want to rip my hair or give him a good punch.

Must I always be associated with the faith-healers and the charlatans? Couldn't I have stuck with a safe teaching career?

Maybe I should call myself a life coach. Business-suit level healing, respected and corporate. Mystery stripped right out. Coach. You can do it, if you a) pray harder b) try harder, c) pray harder. See? Built in. Muscle it up, get a grip, make a list.

Try, try, little soldier.

That's not it. *That's not*, as T.S. Eliot once said, *what I meant at all.* The clincher, the nugget of truth, the buzzing bee is: I am associated with this group. Period. Is Starella different from the store who jacks their profit or the kid who plagiarizes? What if — and this is a stretch, based on the self-made image — she has helped someone? What if the psychic who charges $2,000 an hour (*yes, there are a few*) still has a pure heart?

Who am I to judge? Not me, but I do. The image of a typical Tarot reader is cemented in society. The circus freak. The accent. You know who: the mumu-wearing, triple-divorcee with the 3-packs-a-day husky voice promising fame, fortune and love in one easy reading.

Then there's me.

Yet I could no more put away my cards than I could long to travel, check my email or nap in the sun. It's part of who I am. It's what I do and I'm good at it.

Calista Flockhart plays a Tarot reader in a wonderful movie called *Things You Can Tell Just By Looking at Her*. She shows up at a client's house and waves her deck like an identifying flag as Glenn Close opens the door, expecting the mumu-wearing-triple-divorcee.

Calista spreads out the cards and reveals enough for Glenn to feel despairing and hopeful. Glenn interprets the young man in the reading as her thoughtless lover and hangs on Calista's every word while nervously smoking a cigarette.

I was incredulous. *Calista Flockhart as a Tarot reader?* This was right after Ally McBeal and she was painfully thin. *Who cast her?* There was little substance in her demeanor; in fact, the cards were as large as her head. Her presence was an ethereal wisp against the tight-ass body of Glenn.

And yet and yet and yet. There was yet a lesson for my quick-draw mind. Calista goes home to her lover; a young woman dying of cancer who lovingly calls out from a hospital bed. It's obvious that Calista adores her but as she walks into their tiny apartment, her face is heavy with sorrowful exhaustion.

That scene left me stunned. Did I expect her to be gay? No. Did I anticipate that Tarot was the major source of income while caring for her dying girlfriend? No way. What was the assumed plot in my mind was dead wrong. I figured: surfer boyfriend who relishes her stories while drinking cheap margaritas at an outdoor café and laughing about how they screwed yet another insanely rich and desperate client.

This speaks volumes as to how I view myself as a reader. The paradox, of course, is that I love my work. Except my head can't quite wrap itself around the fact that I actually *do* it.

Do I consider myself psychic? Do I need to? I was so serious as a Christian, so defensive whenever anyone questioned my beliefs. I took major umbrage as if God needed protection from a careless human comment.

Don't be messin' with my God, yo.

Religion brings out my irreverence now. It's good to laugh because it provides a lightness that was notably absent in Christian circles. I mean, *c'mon.* Tarot readings are kooky if you don't understand the art — but the cards don't take offense. They're a tool to be used or put aside. Yet if they aren't given respect, will most certainly shroud their truths.

My cards are light and bright. I didn't start with the Rider-Waite or Thoth as advised because a) I'm contrary and b) they seemed like dark decks. There is already so much darkness in the world; dying lovers, crumbling parents, cold hearts. Many clients *expect* bad news. They anticipate seeing the Death card and hearing their worst fears vocalized.

In my Osho Zen deck, "Death" becomes "Transformation" and "Devil" becomes "Conditioning". These are excellent alternatives. In Tarot, it's how the message is transmitted that allows the heart to stay open. Then the cards can assist in healing.

I get Calista's Tarot reader now; her airy, joyful entrance. She calmly waited for words to come. She avoided soaking up Glenn's frayed energy while keeping her own sorrow at bay.

She was, in other words, able to read.

WHEN IT SUCKS TO BE PSYCHIC

Yep, it's true. It can suck to be psychic.

Imagine pulling cards that show the clear demise of a relationship — then turn to the bright face of your client who just asked about marriage.

Imagine dreaming of cities blown apart: people barefoot and screaming, blood everywhere.

Imagine sitting across from a healer — truly one of the greats — and know that they will turn from their path in bitterness.

Imagine hearing your beloved say words you dread, weeks before s/he utters them.

Imagine feeling the pain of an abused body crying out to be healed.

Imagine speaking to a perfectly nice person whose secrets make your skin grow cold and calls out the warrior in you.

Imagine hearing a client's unspoken question of whether to live or die, then watch them walk away without an answer.

Imagine sensing lies and deception even while in line at the grocery store.

Yep. Some days it sucks to be psychic.

TO SEE WHAT YOU'D RATHER NOT

One of the best ways to hold up a Tarot reading?

Doubt.

Please note: this does not mean to ignore your intuition.

This means to solidly doubt what I tell you.

See, what I do is see. I'm a see-r.

Really.

If you don't want to see what I see, please don't ask.

One of my gifts is being able to view a person I've never met and gain an accurate emotional assessment within minutes. Maybe it's from a chaotic childhood that quickly honed my observational skills. Maybe it's my Scorpio rising. Either way, I'm able to see dark corners that escape friends and lovers. This is a prime reason why CEOs love working with me.

The cards don't lie and I trust what they reveal. I have no reason to believe otherwise.

You can't fool the Tarot. It's very difficult to hide in the cards when you approach them with even the slightest respect. If you are deceiving yourself, the cards will show this. Tarot is a mirror which reflects back our inner landscape. It's amusing when clients are startled by the accuracy. They intuitively choose the cards; I'm merely the interpreter.

A client asked for deeper insight about a close relationship that had suddenly ended with angry recriminations. Believe me, I hate ragged ends. Loathe 'em. Give me resolution or give me resolution.

This client wanted to know why it shook down the way it did.

So, I drew cards on the friend. I said, "Focus as I shuffle. Picture them."

I laid out three to begin. Boom, boom, boom. All reversed, swords flying. Aching unhappiness and anxiety. Wandering eye.

When I revealed this, my client shook their head. "No way. That's not who I know. They have a perfect relationship. You should see them!"

Well, I just did — but how do I convince my client, as the immediate need of a perception adjustment proves too much?

The perfect relationship usually is not. We know this, right? What we idealize falls far short of what we imagine to be the truth.

Why then do we still build these pedestals?

Perhaps we need to believe in perfection to fill the messy gaps of our own lives.

Everyone's got mess. Dirty closets. Trust my cards on that. Sometimes who you think you know isn't the person I see.

When a "perfect marriage" between two dear friends of mine fell apart, we were all emotionally devastated. It deeply hurt because our circle held up their marriage as the one to emulate. I learned then that you never really know what goes on behind closed doors, even with people you love and trust.

It took a few long moments before my client revealed some truths that solidified the wandering unhappiness so apparent in the cards. It was as if my client couldn't accept the dark side of their friend because something would then crack: a light that illuminates our shared experience.

In other words, our propensity to fuck up time and time again.

To be on one end of the sword or the other.

Use common sense. Be discerning. Ask questions. But when a truth comes up that you don't want to face, try not to project onto your reader.

We're not trying to hurt you. We're just trying to open the window.

WHEN A READ GOES SOUTH

Sometimes there will be the occasional client who throws you off your game.

This is a good thing.

I gave a session to a new client. As she spread out the Celtic Cross, I felt pretty confident zooming in, crafting the story and situation.

At least what I thought was the story and situation.

The way I "read" is a witches' brew of intuition, card knowledge, stream-of-consciousness, stories and when appropriate, an off-color joke and swear to spice it up.

Usually, I prefer to start rolling without too many comments from the client. So, I rolled with this particular session and thought she was right there with me.

But something wasn't grooving, even with her regular nods. I could feel it.

I paused and asked, "Does any of this relate to you?"

She looked up and said, "Ah, no. Not at all."

Definitely not what you want to hear ten minutes into a 30 minute read.

Maybe I should have checked in sooner. Maybe that cup of coffee was not such a good idea. Maybe too much confidence was placed on what I thought was her story.

Maybe, maybes.

I've been reading cards for nearly a decade. I've done sessions for many thousands of people. Still, a faint flush of embarrassment bloomed deep in my stomach. The little voices of uh, oh . . . I really fucked this one up. She's going to think I'm a total fraud.

Truth be told, I immediately wanted to say, *Maybe this wasn't right.* Like a disastrous blind date, but with a Tarot reader. Shrug it off and move on. Save face.

Too often in my own life, I've left without following through. Didn't return calls. Took the easy way. Avoided conflict.

This isn't a public display of self-flagellation. Growth is everything.

So is professionalism.

My work is based purely on reputation. That means staying with a difficult read. That means taking a breath and stepping back to the original card. It means re-connecting with the client even in the midst of embarrassment.

It also means acknowledging once again that I am human and not meant to save the world. I'm very human, and doing the best I can with my gifts.

All's well that ends well. The cards opened in a fresh way that enabled me to integrate them with the obstacle at hand. My issue? I made the picture too small for the question.

She left with a smile – and a tip. Above all, I was proud that I stayed present for her.

SOME LIKE IT COLD

"Tell me more," he said, sitting back. "Give me details. Past, present, future."

This was his way, he informed me, of establishing trust. To see how much I knew without him saying a word.

This is what's known as a *cold reading*.

Some clients want me to immediately fill in their story. They compare my type of skills with other readers who gave specific details of their lives. They want to sit back and see if I'm a fraud. This is their gauge.

Fair enough. It's not my favorite type of reading but hey, if we're gonna work together, we're gonna work together. I can do a parlor trick or two.

The real question is: even if I knew specific details of what happened to you as a child, does it enhance the reading or weigh it down?

My strength is being a see-r. Seeing the potential. There is usually one possibility at the moment that shines brighter than the others. When I "see", I often get visions of the client in that particular picture. Again, that's only one picture of many.

Another strength is that I can easily tune into a client's spirit if they are open. The cards help confirm what I already sense, though the client always shuffles and cuts the deck. It's their energy I want on the cards, not mine.

I give the past its due but keep the reading moving forward. The cards always show what needs attention, healing and release. It's more difficult when a client clamps down on their history and resists change. Or if they purposely stonewall or throw a red herring into the mix. That's when you see a ton of reversed cards.

It's easy to fall in love with our story and not grant other ways of being. Re-live rather than transform. It's an interesting balance: telling our story to encourage evolution — or telling our story to watch the gerbil run.

I did the cold reading but offered only a few specific details. I did see the major early trauma and how it affected him now — but didn't plumb the depths for the entire session. That's why there are many good therapists out there.

The past is there to inform — not direct — the present.

I specifically work in generalities. I'm not the type of reader to hand everything to the client. This is where my former life as a teacher comes in handy. We work at it together like a project. A life project. Transformation is where it begins — again.

If a clients trusts you, they'll fill in the relevant details. The beauty of sitting with a stranger is that I usually feel like we've met before. I'm skilled enough to create a safe environment in which they can open up and allow the reading to naturally unfold. When they are ready to transmute the poison of their past into a healing balm, that's when my work hits a magical high note.

You know what you have? he said at the end. *You have a client now. And a brother in this work.*

THE TRUTH OF THE TAROT

"You must hear everything," a client said. I nodded in reply.

That's why I'm the Lynx, the keeper of secrets. Sensitivity is essential in conveying the truth of the Tarot — which is always flexible, always changing based on our decisions. The cards uncover the complexity of the issue and plug a direct line into my intuition. The success of a session is based on how much a client is open to receive. That's why a reader must be humble and translate the message with integrity.

Stay open. Stay honest.

This isn't to say that every client of mine joyfully skips out after a reading. Some resist the message revealed in the cards. Often they will later admit their unwillingness to change when faced with a known truth. Life unfolded as the cards predicted — and helped them to practice flexibility.

Prediction is just another way of seeing what we already knew.

Tarot reflects our inner landscape like a mirror — and very few possess lives of constant equilibrium (*and if you do, I want to know your secrets.*) The cards offer an array of potential — some stronger than others. Always a choice. To listen. To ignore. To act upon.

When I see a client suffering, I so wish to give them ease. Regardless, I must remain within the vision and offer it in truth.

How do you know if it is true?

There's freedom — ultimate freedom — in the message, even if the truth hurts.

THE *YEAH, BUT . . .* CLIENT

On a rare occasion, a *yeah, but . . .* client will appear. They tend to be an intuitive practitioner and run in metaphysical circles. I am especially wary of this type of client, as they can be — how should I say? — prickly. Though I am known as a direct person, I step with care during our reading.

A client who was active in the psychic community wanted advice on how to expand her biz. This is a common question, as many wish to share their gifts full-time *and* pay their bills.

I've found that it's easy to believe that we want to live the life of our dreams, follow our bliss and swan-dive off the cliff of uncertainty . . . but the reality is, reality.

You know, the one we hold with a death grip in our minds.

As I offered my mix of practical suggestion and guidance, a relentless stream of *yeah, but . . .* blocked every sentence.

Yeah, but . . . *I can't live my bliss because everyone around me needs help.*

Yeah, but . . . they need me to save them.

Yeah, but . . . they can't survive without me.

Yeah, but . . . if I'm not breaking my back, what becomes of me?

Yeah, but . . . I hear what you're saying, I respect it but . . .

Yeah, but . . . how can you expect me to not help my partner/child/friend?

Yeah, but . . . I want to follow the Creator of the Universe but I need health insurance.

Yeah, but . . . I need a real job that pays the bills.

On and on. It's a challenge because I'm not there to convince. I give what I'm told in the moment, the movement — and when it is met with resistance, I stop. I observe. I try not to fix, as is my tendency.

Between you and me? *Yeah, but* clients are a total downer. Seriously.

It's unfortunate that healers are full of excuses as to why we can't live our bliss, as if it can only be obtained through our limited beliefs (i.e., *I can do this if I have a partner who supports me, if my kids are gone and a job that gives health insurance, etc . . .*)

This is why so many healers burn out. Not from clients, but from their own resistance.

Let's admit it, okay? We resist being happy. We resist throwing ourselves into the arms of blind faith, the older we get. We resist the messages that come through moments of synchronicity or a smack upside the head. We think we know what we're doing — *I need to do a, b, and c so bliss can come* — and build a plan accordingly. When life starts to tighten around that plan, we look for someone to give us permission, so that we can resist it!

Did my client walk away satisfied? She joked around with the staff but who really knows what she thought of our session? Was I too hard on her? Should I have sugar-coated it? We are sisters in this work but in the end, it's completely up to her to drop that conjunction and say *yes.*

IT'S ALL IN HOW YOU SAY IT

The work I do isn't about parlor tricks or dazzling someone with spiritual knowledge. It's about conveying the particular message for the client as simply and articulately as I can. Everyone is unique in the way that they receive.

It takes many sessions to hone this skill — even psychic work is all about practice. My years of teaching help so much in this regard. It's in the tone of voice and careful choosing of words, while sensing how that person will receive the message without offense. Sometimes I'm more direct, other times gentle. I may give more details or let the client figure it out. Though it doesn't happen often, I've kept certain info to myself because their spiritual task is to find a way through the darkness. A session can be quite the dance — that's why I always ask for help!

I've had personal readings which shocked me with their utter tone-deaf conveyance. I once received a session from an astrologer who asked me to list things that I wanted in my life. I answered, with some vulnerability, that I wanted to be loved. *Oh, please. C'mon! That sounds like you want a puppy,* she said. My heart shrank beneath her caustic response and I silently promised that I'd always be more sensitive with clients.

The last thing an intuitive needs is a client shutting down in the midst of a session — and if you are insensitive, there is a large chance that you will lose their business.

Needless to say, I never called that astrologer again.

Fortunately, the majority of my personal reads have been with wonderful intuitives — and I've learned so much about what *not* to do after the few awful ones.

With this in mind, what are the fastest ways a healer can burn out and lose clients?

- Be a know-it-all or have a guru complex.

- Try to heal everyone, rather than wait for them to come to you.

- Be blind to the emotional landscape of your client because you'd rather get the message out. Sometimes they simply aren't ready.

- Believe you are more spiritual than your client.

- Dazzle with your abilities, rather than show a simple humanity.

- Take your gift for granted and lose the spirit of gratitude.

- Blame your "negative" clients for burning you out, rather than admit your role in attracting them.

When you sense a person's spirit without them saying a word, that's when you know you're on track. It's not about hammering home a message. I'm not there to beat a client over the head. I'm not there to create a purpose — even the attempt is a spiritual disservice. I advise. I listen. I tell them what I see, in a manner that is appropriate. I'm not saying that I get it right every time — but I'm improving.

Looking back on my first Reiki treatment so many years ago, I can understand the youthful, careless mistake that any healer can make in pronouncing *a coldness* and *not letting love in*. After doing thousands of sessions myself, I've come to realize it is how words are spoken, not simply wielding the sword of blunt efficiency to speak the truth.

It's practicing acute attention.

Some clients appreciate directness. Some want a metaphoric story. Some respond to personal experience. Words can be uniquely tailored to suit the person. That is where my intuitive abilities shine.

"Coldness" was an unfortunate, thoughtless word. *Coldness* meant: frigid. It negated the hard work in therapy. It brought up long-buried sexual anxiety. Since I wasn't going to see my Reiki healer again, an hour was not enough time to tie the uncomfortable ends dangling between us. Most certainly my wounded heart closed even further.

However, the Reiki healer taught a valuable lesson: the weight of a word. It's crucial to ask our higher wisdom to guide the session. It's not that her words were necessarily incorrect. It was *how* she spoke them that made all the difference.

And I know full well how those words can remain in one's memory.

Be careful with your words. They may be carried for a very long time.

BULLSHIT CON ARTIST PSYCHICS

It cannot be said enough how disastrous some psychics are with their gift.

Absolutely destructive.

Perfectly sane clients have sat across from me, terrified that I will see a "dark spirit" that haunts them. Why? Because some dumb-ass Tarot reader said it years ago. This same reader also said that if they pay x amount of money, they'll clear the spirit from their aura.

What total and complete bullshit.

{Excuse my Aquarian Moon. She's always had a bit of an attitude.}

You may argue that it is simple to see through charlatans. Who ever wants to view themselves as weak? However, when you are brokenhearted and lost in the event of a sudden breakup or vexing questions, it's easy to seek comfort in people who seem to "go beyond". These psychics will reveal details that no one knows — usually with a young client, the easier to deceive — who then trusts what they say as gospel truth.

Remember: energy is energy. A psychic can use it for good or evil. Some of these con artists are truly gifted but lost in greed. They've crossed over to the dark side.

And it is evil, the purest form of disharmony and selfishness, to use your powers to deceive or take advantage of anyone. It reminds me of Jesus' warning that one who harms a child should put a millstone around their neck and drown in the nearest sea. (Matthew 18:6)

Quite frankly, my clients are like children. Vulnerable, seeking souls who entrust their secrets. I am always aware of this. Let's face it: I am my clients. My clients are me. Often scared, joyful, curious, brokenhearted. I get it.

When I fell passionately for a woman in Christian college, I tried to eradicate love by going to a "deliverance session" — the evangelical version of exorcism. The ones who ran the group seemed sincere. They only wanted to usher my lost, gay soul to freedom through Christ. Here I was: 21 years old, a senior English major, Dean's List, well-respected TA.

And totally desperate.

After the three-hour session, they warned that if I saw my girlfriend or engaged in any desire for a woman in the future, I was in jeopardy of being re-oppressed by seven more demons, including the original. (Matthew 12:45)

Do you know how many years I walked around in pure paranoia after this was said to me?

My logical mind could dismiss the warning with effort but my heart, my childlike self, was completely terrified. Terrified I would lose control of my life and be cast in hell. Of course, my love for women only increased after I headed into the world.

Talk about a total mind fuck. Thank you very much.

This is why deceptive words from Tarot readers make me so angry. Yet even these liars can be great teachers for those who can see through their spell. They teach us to strengthen our discernment and learn to comfort ourselves when feeling lost in this world.

Go to a trustworthy psychic. Ask questions. Walk away if it doesn't feel right. Use your intuition, not have it be perpetually asleep until needed.

Trust yourself. Completely. Totally. Eternally.

The ultimate lesson? Don't hand out your credit card to strangers, even if they know what happened in your aunt's convertible at the family reunion when you were 17.

SAYING GOODBYE TO THE CHURCH

Watching the rabid response of the evangelical community to the coming out of Christian singer Jennifer Knapp set off serious triggers. I'm dumbfounded that we're still having this conversation over gay folk and makes the popular usage of the term *genderqueer* all the more enlightening. Say *gay* and conservative Christians go into a righteous tizzy. Why it causes such rage is bewildering — but not really, as they were once my crew. The need to drill the *I'm right, you're wrong* verses from the infallible Word used to make perfect sense. As God's warrior, I loved to fight the good fight.

Don't be messin' with my God, yo.

Jennifer was interviewed by Larry King and *Christianity Today*, one of the most venerated mags in evangelical circles. I gave props to her courage and cringed at the same time. When I thanked her for living her truth, angry Christians piled on top of my comment. My fire started to flame. God knows I wanted to put them in their place then and there.

However, the biggest lesson I've learned about the evangelical community is that there is little room for intelligent discourse. It is more like banging my head against a wall in Morse code. For whatever reason, homosexuality is the *cause du jour* like slavery 200 years ago. Fighting is useless. Why waste the energy? Jesus advised not to throw our pearls to swine. This time, I took his advice to heart.

This trigger dovetailed with a recent trip home to see my father. The church is his life. Having a daughter who's a proud feminist lesbian has been quite a challenge. He worries about my salvation and we never speak of my love life, as he is grieved by both.

I once believed that I had to actively participate in some type of enlightenment for my Dad. To help him see my goodness. I've given up on that fruitless task and now focus on living my life. I'm not going to change him. Ever. His process is that: his. I spent many young years absorbing his issues and confused "the church" with him. Though resurrection and redemption are inspiring, the evangelical machine can pass on by. I have no need for a church that denies the power of women — and realized this anew while spending time with my frail father who recites the same old lines.

The Christian community never felt quite right. I boil it down to the idea of Jesus' love. That's what people were always talking about in church: feeling Jesus' love. Jesus, lover of my soul. God the Father loving his children. The formula never worked. Why? I've always had an antagonistic relationship with my earthly father, plus the feminine aspect of God was widely scorned and dismissed. Jesus' love was frustratingly elusive. When I fell in love with a woman and was told that — in Christian love — they needed to cast out the demonic influences that made me gay, it was the catalyst to my agonizing break-up with the church.

Oh, I tried to stay a Christian. I let them lay their hands on my body to break me of sin. I believed the only way to heaven was through Christ and contentment through marrying a man. I wanted to believe being gay was a choice. Except I was desperately in love and my warrior self said, *No way. I am not losing her to them. I will not die.*

It's a very lonely road leaving the church. Being gay and surrounded by evangelicals meant instant vilification under the pretense of love. *Change, and we'll love you. We hate your sin but love you. Look how you're influencing young children. It's a choice, so be celibate and follow God's Word. Then we'll love you.*

Their kindness was an iron maiden.

I inevitably lost my first love but finally met my soul. The thought of killing myself came uncomfortably close but I couldn't do it. Just like I couldn't become an atheist or even agnostic. I am undeniably connected to the Source of love.

When I see the Christian hatred directed at Jennifer, I feel a protective anger. It's not for the faint of heart when navigating past fearful Christians in the labyrinth of the church.

Not everyone makes it.

Jesus did say the truth will set you free. And no one, not even those who claim it in Christ's name, has a lock on truth. My truth was that Dad and Mom were my church. I chased after their approval in hopes that they could see me. Sadly, that didn't happen — because deep change was required. An expansion of their truth. An acceptance of difference. Or not.

Once, I wanted to be the best Christian ever; to please my parents and that heavenly Father who constantly looked over my shoulder. My struggle with being gay taught me that denying my truth — any part of it — leads to death.

Guess who was smiling the most on *Larry King?* Jennifer Knapp.

A NON-RESPONSE TO THE NAYSAYERS

There will be plenty of people who doubt what you do. This will come as a result of jealousy, a disconnect to their own power, misguided curiosity or religious constriction.

None of this is your problem. It only becomes so when you let it be so.

Who or what you allow in your world is entirely up to you.

Who or what you allow to influence is entirely up to you.

This is power.

This is magic.

This is freedom of choice.

Learn to banish all else.

A psychic friend mentioned that scientists are finally starting to acknowledge the "reality" of phenomena that has never fit into their structured world. This amuses me, since visionaries have carried this wisdom for centuries.

I hope the ancient Sumerians are laughing, too.

Scientist make it real because they verify, justify and quantify it.

Or maybe they're very, very late to the party.

Truth usually comes down to what resonates in us. What feels right. When it doesn't, we often say, *that's a lie. That's untrue* — because it doesn't fit with our viewpoint. It feels uncomfortable. False.

The force of reaction measures the exact weight of a grain of truth.

What do you believe about your abilities?

Do you believe that you are gifted?

Do you believe that you have a place in this world?

Do you believe that your words affect the very fabric of this Universe?

The truth one believes is the truth one reveals.

Start there.

LEARNING TO SEE

Before the first brushstroke of color on canvas, there is an image that swirls in my mind. I carry it for hours or days and then fill up my bowls with water, choose my special brushes and begin.

Rarely does the initial picture emerge as the final piece, yet it is essential. It spurs me on and helps the dream expand. It gives me courage to finish. With writing, I hear words through various voices in my mind. With photography, it's finding the photo within the photo.

It's following the urges of my Muse in total faith, even when I can't see.

Painting helps me swim in color and quiet the incessant think-box for a few hours. I turn on music and dance around my drafting table, staring at the canvas; away, then back. Adding more, learning to see that every alteration unifies the piece. The essence is there from start to finish. A moving meditation.

I always know when a painting is done. It's as if she says, "Okay, that's enough. There's nothing more to add." Rather than tinker, I admire how well the colors blend as they dry.

Perhaps my idealized life will swirl out differently. What I desire will manifest . . . with its own particular flair. In the meantime, I'm learning to see the beauty of right now.

THE VAST LANDSCAPE OF HAPPINESS

If you will relax and begin saying, "Everything in its perfect time. Everything is unfolding. And I'm enjoying where I am now, in relationship to where I'm going. Content where I am, and eager for more," that is the perfect vibrational stance. ~ Abraham-Hicks

That quote got the old noggin' thinking about happiness. Contentment. Maybe it's all a vast landscape, a plateau of extended vision. Nothing hidden.

It's as far as the eye can see. That's the kicker. As far as the eye can see. When we are content with now while desiring expansion, that's when things show up.

Seems like a wacky koan. Edgy wisdom. If you're content, why want for anything?

I get it. Must be a Gemini thing. An insatiable appetite to go beyond the visual.

It's acknowledging deep, intuitive pulls which are different than twitchy decisions that come after eating a giant piece of cake. For example, I adore my life in Vermont. I've slowly and carefully built a loving community. My reputation as a Tarot reader is solid. Vermont's feminine energy — no joke; there are hips and breasts everywhere in the Green Mountains — has healed my tattered heart.

However, there's a pull. What I consider a "big" move. The life-changing kind.

In other words, the cosmic seven year itch.

Thanks to the harsh, endless winters that have taught me to focus on what my body needs — sun, warmth — while appreciating the good life in every season. The beautiful snowy vistas, the quiet, starry nights while huddled desperately around the heater.

Contentment ———> expansion. Release of the chrysalis.

Every seven years or so, I seek a new act to play elsewhere on this beautiful planet. This time around? An urban oasis where I can sell my car and get back to being somewhat of a city girl. I'm visualizing a place that holds the *essence* of Vermont. A place like Portland, OR — and I've always said that Portland is the big sister of Vermont. Home-grown. Transitory: the ultimate spiritual vibe. Hippy-crunchies — gotta have them. Diversity. Huge trees. The pervasive smell of roses. The spectacular coast. It's far too rainy for my liking — but every place has its compromise.

Whatever the landscape, it's finding grace in the release of now without burning bridges. To extend and touch the mystery with no apology necessary.

From love to love, the harvest of movement.

The grace of endings. The best kind, as there are no real goodbyes.

Happiness, the endless plateau. The richness of ancient ground — all of the lifetimes — and the tablecloth of desire with which to drape over the landscape.

What's next? Who knows? But isn't it exciting?

ON COMPETITION OR LACK THEREOF

A client asked what they should do about a fierce competitor.

First thing is to stop using that word, I replied.

Some may argue that a little healthy competition never hurt none. That may be true — but like me noshing on bags of potato chips this week, healthy can turn deadly in a heartbeat.

There are plenty of fabulous healers. Amazing Tarot readers. Writers whose words gleam in golden light.

No one is my competitor because no one is me, unless you clone me . . . and I hope she's very Zen. No one heals like me. No one reads cards like me. No one possesses my particular *joie de vivre.*

Where's the competition? Oh, yeah. My clone — but she's very Zen.

Words have power. We know this, right? Words have tremendous power: to heal, tear down, welcome in.

"Competitor" conjures up feelings of lack that lurk around our otherwise positive minds. It whispers: *There's only enough for one of us here. I must defeat you. Find out your tricks. Be better than you before you screw me.*

How can I be better than anyone else when no one else is like me?

The more energy we put into aggressively dominating another, making them the robber who comes at the moment we've stopped being hyper-vigilant, guess what is our return?

Like attracts like. Energy is energy. It's what we do with it that matters.

We live in a sport and war-obsessed society. Notice how many idioms — "he's a fighter", "grab a portion of the market", "join forces", "what's your game plan?" — are cast about in a day. This emanates from a masculine-dominated view of the world (*Art of War*, anyone?). This is neither a good or bad thing. Fab if it works for your business. However, I'd be worried about your exhaustion level.

Constantly being on the defense leaks out precious, non-discriminatory energy. The more you imagine a competitor winning, the more you'll fear humiliation. Be seen as the loser.

How much of this stuff goes back to gym class?

Competition is an illusion. No one has your particular mojo and sparkling personality. If you continue building your business — and life — with as much integrity as you can muster, people will desire collaboration rather than "take you down for the count." Conversely, they'll also be the first to sniff out any falseness and middle-finger attitude.

Being genuine reaps eternal rewards.

Sure, there will always be a few who resent your success and envy your freedom. I prefer to see them as frustrated artists whose projections have nothing to do with me. When my fearful voices bubble up — *she's better/cooler/richer* — I return again to the shining self that beams out every day. There's so much freedom in knowing that there is nothing to steal because we are infinite creators.

You don't have to be anyone else because quite frankly, you aren't.

No one brings it to the table like you do — and people will then find your brilliance absolutely irresistible. Maybe even those frustrated artists will be clients in the future. Strange things happen when magic is afoot.

That's true richness. Game over.

LET THIS BE ENOUGH

What if our purpose is to have no purpose?

Being a gifted psychic is like being a gifted baker; wholeheartedly devoting your energy to your gift. Allowing natural abilities to flourish and expand. Loving your work — because you love who you are.

What if we take it a step further and say that names really have no meaning? *Healer. Psychic. Counselor. Guru.* In the end, do labels unite or divide?

What if our true purpose is simply to be available?

To show up and say *yes, I'm here* and mean it.

Imagine if everyone thought of themselves as a healer.

Imagine if the great avatars are actually students in disguise.

Imagine that moment of peace you had last week could extend a few moments more.   Imagine the power. It would transform everything.

What if we didn't have a clue for the rest of our lives?

What if this — right now — is finally enough?

LOGOS INCARNATE

I emailed an ex-girlfriend (*yes, we're still friends . . . it's a lesbian thing*) to talk about "brands" since I *loathe* the word but wanted to know what immediately struck her about my website. She's a former whiz publicist who now teaches prisoners — and likes it better.

She scanned the content, then added, *You may be courting something that doesn't want to be monetized or commercialized. If you want to be a brand and go commercial, you may have to make changes. Do your subscribers trust you? That's the platform.*

While her advice was appreciated, "branding" bores me. Most so-called expert websites bore me. What I really wanted to discuss was Logos incarnate. It's been milling around my brain and I asked her thoughts on the subject. With us, it always goes back to God somehow. God, and the stories between us.

Everyone is Logos incarnate, she said, because she's brilliant like that. It's one of the things I admire and find irritating in equal measure. *Each of us is a word that G_d speaks into the world that has never been spoken before. We are each a new word. Word made flesh. Sign made flesh. It can't be bought and sold.* She admitted that she was paraphrasing, which made me feel better.

Immediately, I started arguing because that's what we do, the clash of two alpha-female brains after 20+ years. I finally conceded and said, *Well, that's all fine and good but what about my bills?* in a whiny email voice.

And bam! The mark of a truly jaded adult. *What about my bills?*

Isn't that responsibility star so pretty? The good girl star. My fridge door is full of them.

Certain social media gurus warn about intimacy and overexposure on your blog. They push niches and brands. Buy—sell—win, baby. Dominate. You're so bad-ass.

This isn't the place to find your brand. Fuck brands. Fuck niches.

Call me a diarist, if you must. This is how my pen rolls. Fleshing out Logos incarnate. What does it mean to step concretely into life, find comfort in this form, this name — the ultimate branding — only to leave it behind in another 30+/- years?

Life becomes simpler in the 40s. Those old thorns don't hurt as much. The names don't matter. Success? Fame? Whatever. When it shakes down, my greatest fear is that these boxes of words will end up in a virtual drawer. A goddamn waste of time.

Despite the angst, the only word I care about is the Divine one given to me.

To carry the word into each lifetime, translating as well as I can.

Drive traffic to your website? I couldn't tell you — other than help you uncover the rarest of jewels: your own Logos incarnate.

Your unique, original voice with the prescience of the ages.

Mystical visions? Great.

Prophecies? Bring it.

An amazing gluten-free coffee cake? Email me.

Does it heal? That is *always* the question.

Do your words heal? If so, then I guarantee clients will trust you.

If indeed we are each a unique word spoken by G_d, then we have a singular responsibility to speak it. No matter how many eras and forms go by.

The world needs your word. Literally. Mother Earth heals through your words. That heartbreak of previous generations find peace through your words. Your words release the prisoners, like the secretly gay kids suffering in Christian churches.

May your Logos incarnate be honored, be heard — and your bills be paid. Contact me for your gold star. I might have a few left from my classroom days.

Word made flesh. Words that we can touch. Taste. Feel in our bodies.

The tangible Goddess. Remember, even Kali heals — after the destruction.

My brainiac friend ended with her own wise words:

Logos incarnate. You can't buy and sell it. When you are face-to-face with ___, that actual union will not be bought and sold. There are certain things that resist a marketing plan. You get your doe-ray-needs met, too. You're smart. You listen. You are open to Love's office hours.

See? I told you she was brilliant.

YOUR WORDS A SONG

A word — spoken — travels across the Universe in eternal flight.

Alive. Organic. Endless.

Words shape the very fabric of the Universe. Love, heat, passion, anger. They are the winds that carry your seed. Patience, kindness, reaching further. All this matters.

You matter.

Your words, a song.

Adding note upon note.

It's the stories that make up a life.

Not: the age, the years, the gray ignored or washed away.

It's the stories. The women. The orchestrations. Machinations.

The faces and music and brightly lit windows.

The boy who said *no* when you asked him to rollerskate.

The way the trees gave their last breath around the teeth of a saw.

The time you walked past a bloody woman slumped on the ground.

A part of your spirit remained there.

This is eternal life. The life in a story.

Even the void casts out a story.

The questions themselves breathe through our words.

This is what continues. The power and strength of a word.

The sorrow of a mother whispering to her child, *live*.

This is the eternal moment.

Life in a breath. Words forming structure.

One of the greatest ways to heal?

Tell your story.

One of the finest ways to teach?

Tell your story.

One of the best ways to release the stranglehold of memory?

Tell your story.

There's no one like you.

And there's no one who can tell your story for you.

But you.

Speak.

Write.

Begin.

All we have is our story.

TO LOVE, TO DREAM
{VIGNETTES OF WATER}

PAST LIVES AND FLUTTERY HEARTS (2001)

"Baby," I said. "Put your head on my breast. How's my heart? What do you hear?"

She lay against my skin for a few moments. "It's fine," she said, patting me. "It's a beautiful heart. Strong. Don't worry. Everything's fine."

I didn't believe her — or any of my girlfriends, for that matter. What in the hell would they know about my heart? There was something terribly wrong that they simply couldn't discern. My heart fluttered at the slightest stress, injustice or even while leaping for joy when love came a-knockin'.

It felt as if she was one beat from death. A stop. No start. Just end.

I wondered if I could love. If I could actually do it. If I'd live to see it.

Or drop right there in the middle of Manhattan while crowds skirted around me with measured affront, as if a coat had been carelessly left in their path. I constantly stressed every New Yorker's private worry: fainting on the subway.

Which actually happened. Slumped right there in the corner of the 6 train like a sloppy drunk on a Saturday night. It was the most peaceful sleep of my life; all eight seconds of it before years of panic came roaring in.

My poor heart. Her palpitations arose in earnest when the upstairs neighbor dropped dead. I heard the clunk, clunk, clunk of the stretcher coming down three flights. Clunk, clunk, thunk. I peeked out. He was wrapped in what looked like a large trash bag as two EMTs navigated the narrow brownstone stairs.

Stop. Start. Stopstart. Start.

Then, of course, 9/11.

It's good to blithely ignore just how scared you are at any given moment. It's good to believe in the illusion of strength. It's even better to have it stripped clean at least once in life. Stripped away, dusty and crying on the ground.

Others reported back on the state of my heart, as I was so distant from her gentle shores. So far from her soft voice that sputtered and stuttered.

I resented the translation.

Nothing but the best for my heart, so an appointment was made with one of the finest cardiologists in the City. She peered over an enormous desk with a quick glance of dismissal, then humored the recitation of my daily life. The OCD pressing of any available aorta. Counting beats and losing count. The gasping breath. The mainlining of Rescue Remedy for a chest that felt repeatedly stung by an electric shockwave.

"You're far too young to have any problems but we'll do an EKG to make sure."

Her blanket statement pissed me off. No one believed that my heart had issues. Like it was made from the finest steel. No sputters; just perfectly tuned echoes. However, the promise of an EKG was enough to give a modicum of peace.

And hey, if anything happened, look where I was.

Watching my heart pump like the most beautiful pistons ever invented was similar to watching the birth of an organ. The solid workings. The bland ignoring of my mind's worries. Pah-pump, pah-pump, pah-pump. *Just doing our job, ma'am.* Pah-pump.

My heart — the working one — had no time for histrionics.

"Your heart isn't stopping," my famous cardiologist said with a large degree of kindness, as my distress leaked all over her Turkish carpet. "It's merely tripping over itself."

That's my heart. One side goes too fast and the other has to run to catch up. A little girl who isn't heard and stumbles after the one who ignores her. The one with other priorities. The one who says no. No. No. Nope. You're a girl. Step back.

"Palpitations are usually triggered by caffeine and stress. Are you stressed?"

What a ridiculous question. Whether or not I'm stressed, I have to handle it. Who else will? Who else pays the bills, feeds the cats, goes to grad school, teaches full time in the South Bronx and makes sure life has some semblance of order? Me. Always me. I will always take care of myself. I've always had to. Always will.

But my heart doesn't quite understand this. She wants caring. Nurturing. She wants rest but we are at least five years away from achieving that goal. We are 30 stories up at a named saint's hospital, chatting in a cardiologist's office full of wood paneling. We must walk out of there with our New York stride — *nothing's wrong, nothing's wrong, what are you lookin' at, huh?* — and immediately down some Rescue Remedy.

We must keep our shit together even as our heart flutters a tiny white flag.

YOUNG LOVE, ETERNAL LOVE

3 of Wands. The Lovers. Page of Cups.

Good start.

"So," she said, leaning forward. "What do you see?" Her cheeks flushed a gentle pink and I could tell that somewhere, she was holding a breath.

Young love, I thought. *So sweet.*

"Looks great. Ooh, a younger man. He wants you there. He's calling you. Lots of love and fire."

She smiled a little Mona Lisa smile.

"Are you sure? Am I gonna get there and then have it fall apart?"

Everything was as smooth as butter in her reading and it delighted me. Rarely is one on love so easy. Usually it's highs and lows. Breakups. Old exs. Anger. Trouble lurking around every corner.

This one was a stroll through a field of daises.

I laughed. "Well, there's no guarantee of anything but you both have the heart of a child. That's the best sign of a long-lasting relationship. What are you waiting for? Go, go, go!"

"Yes," she said. "I think I will."

As she slowly stood from the wicker couch, she said, "I'm in my mid-70s. I've never left this state except for a short visit to see my brother. On a plane. I'm terrified of planes. But I'm gonna do it. I've lived my life for everyone else, and now I'm living it for me. My eldest is in a snit about it but I say, *too bad.*"

"You're my hero," I said, hugging her.

THE BEST THAT CAN HAPPEN

We've been taught to ask, "What's the worst that can happen?"

Why?

To assume the worst. Hope for the best. Land somewhere in the middle.

Why not ask instead, "What's the best that can happen?"

Drink up, dreamer.

Dream, dream, dream.

ALL IS WELL

I furtively hand over the purple package to my brother as we pass each other in the tiny hallway of my childhood home. He accepts it into his huge hands with silent grace.

"Try these," I whisper. "I think they'll help." He's starting to get a cold and I'm skeeved that he'll spray germs all over but it's too late.

Here we are: 38 and 40 year old siblings, whispering over my personal set of *Animal Medicine Cards* because we can't bear to face our father's wrath and attendant lecture if caught. My brother takes the cards into his room and lays them face-down on a flannel bedspread. I can't blame him, nor do I take offense. I'd spent many years de-gaying my speech, relationships and living spaces for the comfort of my parents.

My brother connected with the cards as I knew he would. He's always loved animals and as he grows older, trusts more in his substantial intuition. The woods and ocean have been his comfort and escape. In another lifetime, he was probably an Indian guide or explorer. I'm not sure what sealed his karmic fate for this one; trapped in a ranch house with my parents in the mall suburbs of New Jersey. Must have been a doozy.

Our father never caught on and my brother handed back the cards before I zoomed off to Vermont. He smiled and mumbled, "Yeah, they were good," when asked how it went. My Gemini brother goes off on tangents of his own accord but doesn't do well with direct questions. Typical Gemini.

After three days of disinfection, I reached for the cards in my own bedroom. I missed the animals and kept one card upright as I slept, as they were my protectors in the dreamworld. My brother had thoughtfully clipped the six blank cards that were separate from the rest of the 53. In my lazy way, I had merely flipped them and made sure not to mix and match during a read. Too many blanks were too much unknown for me.

I asked, "Who wants to come with me tonight?" and pulled a card. It was blank with the word *Love* scrawled in smeary black ink over the empty shield.

The word startled me, like waking up groggy and not remembering my name for a discomfit period of time. There were other blank shields with my written phrases such as *Trust* and *All is well* — but *Love?* Nope, not mine. I even turned the waxy card over to see that the pen had nearly pressed through. It was then I recognized my brother's cartoonish handwriting under the smear.

My brother: the brawny, silent type. The loner. The one with such a sensitive heart that he spent years in and out of a fishing boat to brood over women (though adopted, we share that brooding trait). My brother with the broken teeth and dark scowls that kept people at a distance wrote *Love*, knowing I'd find it someday. Maybe he knew me better than I thought.

I shuffled through the rest of the deck and found more scrawls. *Relocate* and *Wealth*. Both of us were broke and considering a move to New Mexico, so those words weren't a surprise. Our Hispanic roots were pushing up, seeking the sun.

And which card did he first pull out of the deck?

All is well.

LOVE, LOVING LOVERS, ME.

I fell in love with a Tarot reader once. Man, was she hot: one of those gorgeous Black Irish girls with jade green eyes and thick raven hair (*enhanced*, she later admitted). And a Taurus. Don't get me started on Taurus women. They are irresistibly attractive but my heart has been smashed enough by their bull heads that a huge breath is required before jumping into their bed.

But jump I will, knowing better.

This Taurus wore a gold ring that instantly neutralized any future magnetism. At first, I didn't even notice her. We were studying local healers in Mexico and the days were jammed with workshops. With 20+ women in our group, there were plenty of people to meet.

The brightest of full moons shone down one night early on. I leaned against a rock wall that ringed the common and peered out from the shadows.

A woman started spinning in the grassy field, a braid shaped like a hot pretzel around her head. She sang and swirled, unconcerned that people were watching and thinking she had a pretzel on her head.

"Who's that?" I asked my tent neighbor who also propped up the wall.

"Oh, that's Black Irish girl." With that, she gave a yawn and said goodnight.

Hm, I thought. *Very interesting.*

The dancing spiral sauntered up, a graceful bull flushing out my clandestine operations. Soon after, I'd discover that she was not only psychic but telepathic. Oops.

We exchanged a friendly hello before wandering off to our respective beds. The following morning, she mentioned that she was a Tarot reader as we traveled on the bumpy road into town. She wore the most outrageous outfit, all flouncy frills and a giant hat you'd see at the Kentucky Derby. Her arm flung over the seat and hovered right above my thigh. The arm with the ring. All the barriers in place. Her voice pierced like a horn bellowing from an old Vermont fire station. I worked my charm to the hilt with total irreverence. She laughed and laughed.

That's when the energy shifted. It was her laughter that changed everything.

I asked about her success with Tarot readings. She had a hopping practice with clients who booked months in advance. She was *known*. I was slightly envious but much more interested in finding out how she read. It was like visiting all those healers upon my arrival in Vermont. I was fresh and baby-new. It was time to learn.

I shyly asked if we could barter mutual readings but then became really nervous when she said yes. I wasn't ready to read for someone of her stature in the Tarot world.

What if she thinks I suck? What if I forget the card meanings? Shit.

To be honest, I had no idea how effective she was as a reader. Anyone can think they're good but the proof is in the pudding. I'd find out soon enough.

We didn't read each other until after we slept together. *What happens in Mexico*, I nonchalantly pronounced, *stays in Mexico*. She was married to a gay guy, right? Weren't they on the edge of divorce? Didn't she nearly say she loved me when I stopped her mid-sentence, frightened by her bull strength?

Didn't I try to stop it?

I'm getting ahead of myself. That night, a local woman with liquid hips taught us how to salsa. If you want a preview of how a woman will be in bed, watch her eat — or dance. Especially salsa. It's a mesmerizingly languid sensuality.

Black Irish Girl and I moved towards each other, hips angling for contact. The group surrounded us. Close, then apart. She went dancing later in town as I headed to my tent. Didn't even brush my teeth; that's how tired I was. Fell asleep with fuzzy teeth, three layers and heavy wool socks.

I suddenly shot up in bed and checked my watch. 2:30. Why in the hell was I up at 2:30? There was still an hour or so before the roosters. I flopped back down and waited for sleep to descend.

"Buenas noches."

I flew up again, startled. The voice was far enough away to be unrecognizable, yet close enough that I knew it wasn't an angel.

The zipper on the tent slowly began to unclench. An arm sheathed in red folded the rest down. Black Irish Girl.

"Hi . . . what? What are you doing here? How was dancing?"

"Dancing was good." She boldly lay right next to me and pulled the covers over her dress. "How are you?"

"Woke up from a dead sleep and don't know why."

She smiled. "I was calling you, silly. Silently. In my head." The faintest aroma of sweet rum lay on her lips.

God, the one time I forget to brush my teeth . . .

"This is what you wanted, isn't it?" she whispered, climbing on top.

Who was I to argue with a bull?

Later that week, she gave readings to a few courageous souls. You'd need that particular quality as she was terrifyingly direct. A force of nature.

13 cards were laid out in a spread based on the astrological houses. It seemed very complicated and I asked her to explain each position. She was patient but once into a session, did not like anyone interrupting her flow. Clients were firmly instructed not to say a word when they entered her home.

She started to give a reading with that horn voice to my tent neighbor, for whom I felt an instinctual protectiveness. Bam! *This is going to happen to you in 2 months.* Bam! *Watch out for that person.* Bam! *Let's look at your health.* She was like the Emeril of Tarot readings. If you couldn't handle it, by all means get the hell out of the kitchen.

Black Irish Girl was, in a word, rough. She revealed that it would be a trying time when my neighbor returned home and I saw the life force drain out of her face as she bravely tried to absorb the news.

Bam! *Ask this person for help*, she finished. *Don't be afraid. They'll come through.*

Our group fell back on various beds, exhausted and secretly grateful that this wasn't our read. Even Black Irish Girl looked a little stunned and sorry. *It's going to be okay*, she said to my tent neighbor who was deciding if it was all a crock of shit.

When Black Irish Girl gave me a session, my innards clenched. All of my psychosomatic fears swept into the room, awaiting their audience. I almost said, *Hey, don't bother. Let's go back to my tent.* Her reading was similarly brutal and specific enough that when certain things came true later, I said, *wow*. It was vague enough that if they didn't, I could easily forgive her. She said be extra careful with my taxes as a form was missing (right) and that I'd soon be moving into a house that was owned by a woman. It wouldn't be perfect but perfect for me at the time (correct, and it sold within months.)

She also revealed that my budding Tarot business would be extremely strong in a few years. I'd be known.

This is your thing, she said. *Do it.*

When I read for her, a natural confidence emerged once I fell into the cards. This harkened back to a teaching career where I'd dazzle with my bullshit even if I was a nervous wreck in front of a roomful of cynical students.

In her cards I saw marriage, the children, the set up. I saw the inevitable anger and dissolution. The new love. I imagined that place as mine. Easy to do when you want it there.

Death appeared at the food court table as we waited for our planes. Though we were ultimately headed to the same state, somehow I knew we'd never see each other again. My beautiful heart was breaking in hopeful worry as it always does when saying goodbye to a lover in an airport. It never gets any easier.

Transformation, right? I said, pointing at the card. *Maybe a new life with a woman who has kids?*

Maybe, she said. She smiled but I knew. I always know. It's the burden and the gift of being an intuitive. I know. It was death, pure and simple. The final separation. The final cut.   *Goodbye.*

I bought three bottles of liquor after arriving home in a lame attempt to get drunk but the money would have been better spent on dollar scratchies. I downed a few rum and Cokes but worried about the caffeine content as I cried on my kitchen floor looking, for all intents and purposes, like a droopy knight on a spotted chessboard.

I mumbled my well-worn mantra. *No matter what, I will always be okay.*

Try, try, little soldier. Try.

The slatted windows in my parents' basement rose above grassline and gave me comfort as a child, though the dank space smelled like wet gravestones. It was my escape from the loud voices that regularly rose and fell through the vents. I'd walk the treadmill or leaf through ancient National Geographics on a green leather chair that bit into my legs. I did pullups on the rusty steel beam as I was the only girl in Little League, after my heart was crushed when told a professional football career was unthinkable.

Over the years, my oldest brother served as my unpaid trainer.

"Throw the ball harder," I'd yell as we played catch. "As hard as you can."

I was so afraid of smashing my teeth again but held the glove right in front of my face. My brother threw the ball so fast it took the echo a few seconds to catch up and crack against the blue house behind me. My palm stung like running my fingers against a picket fence — but I caught it.

"Nice job," he'd say. Then we'd do it all over again. *As hard as you can.*

If you'll allow me a little 10 of Swords drama . . . oh, the years I've suffered over women. Before, during and after coming out.

My life *is* the Lovers card, both upright and reversed. Lesson exemplar.

Like Death, VI Lovers is widely misunderstood and taken at face value, not unlike a cheerleader who's also a Rhodes scholar. When it pops up in a reading, faces brighten, lungs exhale, all's well. Well . . . not quite. The Lovers represents inner harmony, long before that real lover appears.

It requires release for gain. Venus is hardcore, baby.

The Lovers card helps us — and few ever want to hear this — to remove disharmonious relationships. V Hierophant (blessing, spiritual quest) and VII Chariot (fast changes) surround the Lovers in sequence. The Tarot gives opportunities to evolve long before XIII

Death arrives. It allows us to make the choice, as Death carries a really big sword and isn't afraid to use it.

Love, loving lovers, me. If I could distill the thousands of readings I've done over the years into a pure liquor, it would be 98.9% love proof. To the credit of my clients, the questions are not simply, "Does he love me?" or "Is she going to leave?" They're wrapped in a complex story long in the making. Unraveling it in one session can be a challenge.

Will I be loved by another? Will they stay? Can I do this?

A force drew me to my greatest loves with an irresistible pull. Oh, I tried resisting. If I had let my intuition speak, she would have said, "There's a reason for this, Missy. Go with it."

There was no tapping in, however. No letting go. I controlled the shots, the pace, the come-ons. One woman I dated said, "You're like a window with a shade. You open the window but pull down the shade. Or you're always right at the door. You never give me a chance to be at the door."

The window, shade and door were open but Black Irish Girl had already left the room. She had to. Intuitives can't fool themselves if they're completely honest. Life's inexorable pull was at work and all we could do was submit. Death did her duty and cut the final cord.

You'll be a great success one day, she said. *Remember me.*

I do.

WHAT IS LOVE?

I've always been an observer. I am also blessed with the memory of an elephant that serves to protect and fillet me all at once. My heart, however, is the more mysterious element.

I don't really understand love.

The "I would die for you" sacrificial kind was infused throughout my Christian upbringing. Love has always equaled suffering. Jesus died on the cross for our sins in the ultimate act of love. Bloody, wounded Jesus.

I'd like to think that it was an act of love when my mother, after nine long months, released me prior to a touch against my skin. Maybe it was all selfishness. Protection. Maybe Jesus simply tired of Earth. Maybe my mother saw it as act of Catholic charity with sin and judgment looming in her mind. Maybe it was the best she could do.

Perhaps what we call love is merely an innate need to suffer.

How much of truth is an illusion? How much of this idea of love is created?

How much of life is edited to highlight the heroic parts?

Without our stories, we are nothing. Or perhaps right at the beginning.

What *is* love?

Christianity teaches us to admire and emulate the suffering of Christ. To be the martyr in light of an eventual reward. To be scorned for the message. What's that again?

Love one another. Love God. Love your neighbor as you love your self.

There's that word again. *Love.*

What if you don't really know what love is in the first place?

It's a fabulous goal, nonetheless. Of course you'd be laughed at in a world that obsesses over war with everything set up as a competition. *I win. You lose. Mine, mine, mine. All mine.*

The me-me-mes who own everything: the road, the wife, the house, the religion.

This same world that conversely honors dead heroes who suffered for the greater good, then casts a wide net of suspicion over anyone who doesn't act accordingly.

It's easy to draw in actors who will gladly help us play out the movie of our lives: comedy, drama, horror. Then we can say, "See? This is the truth! Told you!" while ignoring the fact that the whole thing can be scrapped.

What is love? Is it possible to know the meaning while astride petty hatred?

Is it possible to be heroic without suffering?

Is it foolhardy to finally leave the warrior behind?

What is love?

Here's an interesting experiment. Ask anyone their meaning of love. You may hear phrases such as: *giving yourself to another, sacrifice, that fuzzy feeling, life-long commitment, I adore her, think of someone other than me* — as if we share a selfish gene and must train ourselves to be more kind. Is this love, or acting out the vision of what we consider to be a good person?

What is love? It's a tricky koan. Of course, Jesus' words come flooding in: *love God and your neighbor as your self.* He brings it home to me. How I treat my self is the example of how I would treat God — which is a toughie, since it uncovers another question: *who is God?*

Bring it back to self. Is this love? Absolute care for this beautiful body. This wondrous, squishy being. Love for my precious consciousness.

It's a start.

What *is* love?

Perhaps love is being awake.

Perhaps love is being fully alive.

Perhaps love is a word that doesn't even touch the hem of the actual expression.

IMAGINE THIS (DREAM)

Imagine ourselves as a medium for our wounds.

Calling them out.

Healing them.

Releasing them.

Imagine the freedom.

Imagine.

YOU, ME & OUR INNER TYRANTS WALK INTO A BAR

It is so very easy to be proud, hard and selfish.
So easy — but we have been created for better things.

~Mother Teresa

Proud, hard and selfish — against the world? Easy to recognize. Let's face it: if we have a spoonful of consciousness, we know when we act like assholes.

How about proud, hard and selfish — against my own self?

To trust that inner critic who says, *Raven, why aren't you more Zen? Let me tell you why. You're never going to get rid of that temper. Who do you think you're foolin', honey? You constantly doubt yourself. You're never gonna find a girl. Besides, you'd only fuck it up.*

You may know these voices and give shelter your own tyrant — "rant" being the operative word — who rules the roost in some dark corner of your spirit. If not, please start writing your bestseller and grant me an immediate consult.

I've tried rooting him out — yes, it's a male voice. I've tried all sorts of witchy things to dispel the perfectionist. He just laughs, hangs around and shakes his head.

What's the one word that settles the angst?

Love.

It's the hardest spell in the book. To whisper words like a loving mother to my pained spirit. The one who loves me, no matter what.

No questions asked. To not figure it out. Or find a way around. Or run away. Setting the tyrant in his place by saying, *I love myself. I'm doing the best I can. All is well. I'm safe.*

To end with: *I even love you, you old bastard.*

The more I sit with these ideas of forgiveness, the more I see that we never really get rid of anything. We remember. We learn to live with discomfort. We learn what it means to love the self, baby — always the self, first and foremost. We start to catch the old sabotage and reroute the neurosis with a loving hand. We practice gentleness in a way that works with our temperament. We do the best we can.

But girlfriend, it ain't easy.

Still, let's continue down this road together. We've been made for better things.

LOVE IS MY AMBITION

I meet all kinds of people in my social media world. Especially women. Ambitious, passionate women. The ones who have it going on. I lean back in amazement at their ability to shine in whatever genre. I admire the effort to build their brand, roll out products, increase lists and line up gigs. Teleconferences. E-books. Newsletters. Find an agent. Land a big show. Rub shoulders with the metaphysical Illuminati.

Add a kid or two and a partner. Their ambition is breathtaking.

And it is so not me.

Often ambition means: work your ass off. Show how you've brought it to the bone. Their ambition seems to birth from passion — but truth be told, many times I come away exhausted. Where is the ease?

Different strokes, folks. Totally understandable. 9-5 never grooved with me. My orbit is around the dreamers, the risk-takers who may never really *make it*. Who may never have *anything to show*. The visionaries who blaze paths for others to discover and call their own.

This idea of ambition in my 40s? Well, that word is close to being retired. The 40s are all about joy and ease if I let them be. The eternalness of life grants me this — and the "reality" of age says, *baby, you're halfway through this particular ride.*

Love — now — love is my only ambition. Ambitious enough for this girl. Let success and acclaim go to others. The rest? It's here. I haven't missed anything. Love: — in love — with this wildly expansive, passionate life.

SAVOR IT ALL

Savor ~

the unexpected kiss.

the warmth of a spring sun, rising high and bright.

the heartbreak you thought you were long over.

the song you loved and forgot until you heard it again.

the irony of a gluten-free pizza.

the .70 royalty check.

the unending goodness of appreciation.

the awkwardness of it all.

Every little thing.

Every little thing.

Every little thing.

Savor.

TO LOVE YOUR DOUBT

There will be times that you question what you do. You'll question this life. You'll question the need for spirituality. Is it all a crock? Maybe.

Maybe there is no life after this one. Maybe there is no magic wand and we are thrust into this existence, cursing or creating stories out of the void. Maybe the best Tarot readers are simply eloquent advice givers. Maybe we are total quacks.

Let the questions be. Don't fight them — but don't automatically buy into them. Pay attention? Yes. It will help to focus again on why you do what you do.

Why do you do what you do, anyway?

If you have a clear answer, stay there. It's enough. The questions don't take away from your inner knowing.

This is what I do. This is why.

Most importantly, love what you do. Nothing else matters. If love is present, people can't help but be transformed. They will listen and extend trust.

It's possible to talk a good game — but try to fake genuine care.

There are plenty of times after a session that I doubt myself. It's guaranteed to happen if you read for as long as I have. There are various reasons: an off moment, indigestion, a client doesn't like what they hear, your energies don't match, etc.

Do the best you can. What you say will make sense later on . . . or perhaps it won't. That's okay. If you did the best you could; were open, honest and acutely listening, then understand again that you are human. You are not meant to heal the world. You are not meant to be the missing piece of their puzzle.

You are no one's guru. Be grateful for that.

Love — is a good place to begin. Love for yourself, love for the work and your client. That openheartedness can't be touched if you take the long view of things. It protects you. Doubt is part of the package. It is your Chariot of focused intent.

I never wanted to be a Tarot reader. I wanted to be *something* — but Tarot reader wasn't it. It was cheesy: looked and sounded plain cheesy — and a cheeseball I am not. It surprised me to learn that Jerry Garcia first wanted to be a painter and reluctantly took up the guitar. When he played those unearthly jams, did he ever wish to be transported instead to a gallery filled with his work?

Doubts have their place. Give them room. Those dreams we sorrowfully release do return in their more perfect forms at the right time. Jerry Garcia had to let go of his idea of "artist" to become one. I wanted to be a vet. Psychologist. English professor. A writer. I am all of those things. I am the teacher delving into symbols, colors and meaning. I'm the counselor when people reveal their struggles. I am the vet giving Reiki to animals. If I had locked myself into one arena, it would have simply choked my gifts.

But that old question remains: isn't there something better, more suited, more naturally glamorous? A perfectly tailored career.

My desire for recognition wasn't from Tarot — but so it is. I'm a gifted reader and devoted to my work. It's another coyote joke that Tarot cards are my stage — and not teaching from an elevated podium at a snooty college or penning the great American memoir. The term "Tarot reader" has the mystique factor that triggers interest or outright hostility. Quite frankly, I don't care for the attention but am making my peace with reading cards.

It takes our good friend hindsight — who is always late — to reveal why things work out the way they do. It takes grace to forgive ourselves for not living the life our younger dreams imagined.

When it all shakes down, it's about expression. Expression of the self and the ancient wisdom that continues to guide and push us forward. Perhaps our souls have gone through the eternal washing machine for enough cycles that this time around, our lives billow out. To believe in our purpose with a full heart.

Expression beyond names: through this mouth, these feminine fingers and olive skin. This soul who has seen so many lifetimes of love, heartbreak, war and ruin. This soul who has wandered far and wide, looking for her perfect mate. This soul who understands the pain of death and the ultimate agreement of accepting the illusion.

All this to be expressed again and again throughout endless lifetimes.

And love, the greatest of all mysteries. Love: to let in and watch it flow out again. To love our certainty — and our doubt — as a whole being.

This time, invite her to the party. Ask her to stay.

A SENSE OF WONDER

I've stopped reading books on how to find God.

All that I need to know about God is revealed through Nature, if I'm willing to listen. The magic elixir? A sense of wonder. It's impossible to experience la dolce vita without it.

Clients ask: how can I connect to my soul? What's my higher purpose?

Honestly, it's not for me to answer. I wouldn't even presume — but those are some of the greatest questions one can ask.

Often I cite the example of Siddhartha. He fruitlessly sought enlightenment for years before returning to his teacher Vasudeva. After listening to his heartbreak, Vasudeva encourages him to spend time by the river. It is there, sitting on the bank, when Siddhartha finally hears "Om".

Me? I don't exactly hear "Om" in my Adirondack but I listen. I listen, even when my interior lands rage from somewhat peaceful to downright chaotic. I listen to the frogs trill and the peepers peep. I listen to the whine of the mosquitoes around my ears. I listen to the birds gossip before bed and the wood thrush sing the last note. I hear cars approach and coyotes chattering — all to fall silent if I wait long enough.

I remember to ask: "What do you need, heart?"

My youth was spent seeking a God who floated beyond this wicked world. The map of the Bible only served to confuse. I prayed, "God, I want to know you. Show me how."

How could I find Him as my sinful heart was *deceitful above all things*? The voices around me preached: You're not trying hard enough to love God. Try harder.

No one taught wonder, except for the complex King David and his lovely psalms.

The funny thing is: the clues were everywhere. Even Jesus hinted at it when he said, "The Kingdom of God is within you."

Who eventually arrived when I stopped praying that prayer? Love.

Love for my self in this precious body and love for this amazingly beautiful world.

In essence, love for the Divine.

Somewhere in all of the listening comes a greater awareness. Sometimes even peace. Usually it is revealed during the "tween" times before dawn or twilight; the time where spirits pass easily through this world. This sense of wonder — when regularly nourished — makes the natural world a necessary bloodline running through my life. I'd die without it.

To have a sense of wonder isn't necessarily to know. It's to say: *I believe.*

Besides — anything is magic or bullshit, depending on how you see it.

My mom passed in early 2010 and recently came in a dream. I said, "Hi, Mom! How's heaven?" She telepathically explained that heaven was right next to me. Not above. She swept her arm up and down to signify that it was here. Literally a step away in another dimension.

I can't help but consider that Nature is that link, the "tween" time of our existence here. Nature is where we can more easily understand the life of now and also beyond this form.   Rubbing shoulders with the eternal. Perhaps we are not so separate, after all?

This tweet from a friend pulled it all together: "In Chinese, the character "ren" (human) shows how we are the connection between heaven and earth."

Having a sense of wonder — is the beautiful opening to that portal.

LONELINESS IS LOVE IN DISGUISE

When it came to love relationships in my younger years, I was the master of escape. Piss me off? *See ya.* Want more love? *Later.* I'd make my threats, bag up my things, throw a stoop sale in whatever pre-gentrified 'hood I lived in — and dump the dregs on the sidewalk to watch it all disappear within the hour.

Yeah, cart off the shit. Do my dirty work. See ya.

No one packed a car better than me. Hours were spent negotiating the perfect fit for every box while keeping the rearview clear. I'd thrill in dropping off crates of books to the library and giving items to delighted friends.

My life was the unending stoop sale.

I wanted my relationships to disappear just as easily. I wanted to disappear, but not be forgotten. Of course my exs would fling open the door if I ever deigned to knock again.

So, I'd pack my car and drive. Cape Cod, Colorado, Las Vegas. The Hudson Valley. Back and forth to the City. Always more to see — and plenty of time to perfect the art of longing.

Drink up, dreamer.

One of the more spectacular moves was NYC to Portland after splitting with my long-term girlfriend. I added the dramatic flourish of driving off with another woman beside me.

On that first Oregon morning, I walked outside and stood in the middle of the main drag. Hawthorne. The street was empty and a pink dawn slashed across the buildings. Mt. Tabor loomed in the distance. I had never felt more desolate.

What the fuck am I doing? I said out loud, resisting the urge to get in the Jeep and drive straight back to Brooklyn and the woman whose heart I had shattered.

Clarity can be like a too-salty soup — but you're so hungry, you eat it anyway. The difference? There's a tall glass of water right next to the bowl. All of the packing and organizing and lesbian processing didn't get rid of the one thing that stood beside me.

My loneliness.

I'd love to say that moment on Hawthorne changed everything. But loneliness was a passenger for many more years before I finally and fully recognized her.

Love in disguise.

It takes courage to admit that you're lonely. It takes even more to embrace her, to let her stay, to let her be part of the ride.

ONLY THIS

I love you.

Only this

releases me.

LOVE: JUST FORGET ABOUT IT

I've been reflecting on the arduous struggle called l.o.v.e. as Valentine's Day encroaches. What better time to consider heartbreak?

It's taken me this long — half of my existence — to finally get it about love.

Kinda.

How to attract a perfect partner? Don't ask me — and don't believe anyone who says they do. They're full of shit and will more than likely be divorced in 6 years or less. Or on their 3rd marriage. Or be perpetually single.

Attencion! Here are my earnest words of wisdom when it comes to love — love in its most curvy, luscious form.

Forget about it. Yeah, that's what I said. Forget all about it.

Notice how I'm not saying, *let go*. Those two words should be permanently stricken from the universal lexicon. Who needs more hippy-dippy syntax? Vermont has plenty.

Denied! But I'm kind of saying it. Without saying it.

Love is getting to a point where you don't care whether you're partnered or not because a) your friends have driven you bat-shit crazy with shards of wisdom such as *let go* or *why isn't someone like you with someone like you?* or *love will find you when you're not looking* and you've alienated yourself for sanity's sake and b) you realize that it *doesn't matter*.

We're all headed to the same place, so every minute that passes provides yet another moment to be comfortable with the best partner you can find.

You know who this is, right? You, of course. This intimate matter of the Divine union of souls. Namely, the Divine.

The only relationship worth its salt — and this is a big statement — is the one between your soul and the Divine. Call her God, Great Lady, Nameless Mystery, et al. That union transcends the body. The eternal union. Once there is a groovy flow — or at least a good effort in maintaining that relationship — then will the lovely, fleshy representations start to appear.

The delicious reflections.

They may first appear in dreams. An active dream life is a huge compass as to where you stand in love — and whether you're ready to continue the mutual story that two passionate dreamers bring to "real" life.

Believe me, I've put in my order — one of the longest in the universal kitchen — done the rituals, purified my heart, sang the songs, lit the candles, bowed down and never, ever sacrificed hope on the altar of bitterness and finally said: *I'm done. It's all set up here.*

To want, to need, to crave love? Tricky. A tricky trap.

To adore love, to welcome and delight in her presence? Yes.

Love will still be here when we've exhausted ourselves seeking her. Love isn't found: it just is. Present in the spirit, the beautiful minutiae.

Love doesn't need to announce herself in the body of the beloved. It is quite clear in how much we embrace the beloved moment — with or without a heartmate. How much we willingly give back because we can't help ourselves because life is so good, so full of grace.

What I do know is that I am my lover's and she is mine. I wake with her. I see her everywhere. And when I finally meet that beautiful reflection, may she be as perfect an image of the relationship I already treasure.

A LOVE LETTER

Hey, girl —

I love you. Congrats on graduation. You barely got out alive. Didn't matter that you made Dean's List. Once they discovered you and J, they smelled blood — but you made it. Maybe there is a God who watches over you?

You're having such a hard time. You love so deeply but that sweet and sensitive heart (*don't scoff*) is becoming armor-plated by the day. Shiny silver plates like some confused Joan of Arc. Where to put all that intense passion?

That passion is a gift. That anger your greatest protector. Someday the war will end but it's keeping you alive right now. Someday that armor will grow too heavy and you'll choose a more peaceful path. Right now it's too soft, too exposed. No time yet for peace. You can't let love in. Look what it's doing to you.

I love you. You like it real but it breaks my heart to tell you this: she will leave you. It will take the majority of your 20s to finally accept that it was time to move on. Baby, love *will* triumph in the end. I know that merely twists another angry blade in your heart. I'm sorry. You keep fighting ghosts but know that she's gone.

In fact, there will be three great loves by age 40. Can you believe that? You will love fiercely, imperfectly. They are the ones who will get in — and will inevitably shatter your heart. Know that they love you. They will all return in their own way after the pain subsides.

You changed them, too. You are not forgotten. Your love is not wasted. The anger will pass. This idea about "getting over" someone? It's kind of bullshit. There is such freedom in understanding that love — real love — doesn't die. It just changes. The hardest part is learning how to have the grace to let it change, because change it will. It's a delicate dance and one that will not come easy for you.

Still, there are thousands of miles ahead and the verdant forests you love so well. Find a way to rest. Keep reading Rilke. Write in your journal. I know how troubled your spirit is. I know how strong you try to be. I love you. There will be many people — angels, strangers, mothers and friends — who will step in to help you. Let them.

You're often going to hear *let go* and it will irritate the shit out of you. And you'll run. So, run. This is your Appalachian Trail.

You trust no one. Even her. Especially her. There are so many women to come, so many heart-wrenching decisions ahead. Go where the wind takes you. Crank that Peter Gabriel tape while passing over watery treetops. *Only us.* Cry as you mumble into the recorder, pretending she can hear. Cape Cod, Colorado (a little orange cat will be joining your travels), the Hudson River Valley, Portland, Las Vegas, and the beautiful City you'll never leave . . . until you do. New Mexico, Montana, Vermont. The Canyonlands. The Badlands. Rome, Venice, London. There's so much beauty ahead but your restless heart won't be able to fully absorb it. Not yet.

So, run. Snap those shots. Kiss and touch those beautiful bodies. There are desolate times ahead, the darkest hours — but you are far stronger. You will live. You have the strength of many lifetimes. You know how to do this.

Take it all in. It will heal you. Just remember: it's okay to fuck up.

I love your free spirit. I love how color is your friend. I admire your idealism and loyal heart. I love how you make grumpy people laugh. There's something I need to say, even if you can't accept it: no one will love you as much as I do. No one. I will always be with you, urging you over that hill and around that next corner.

Try to see around those timetables in your head. You're becoming a fine writer. You don't have to be an English professor to prove yourself. Those dreams of travel, working with teens, publishing, speaking? All will come, in surprising ways. Trust me.

Don't settle. Take the time to find out what it means to be who you are. And when you're startled by unexpected happiness, soak it in. *Suck the marrow*, as you like to say. Squeeze that orange. There's no need to justify your life to anyone. You're here and the world is a better place for it.

There's so much beauty ahead.

Love,
Raven

p.s. Here are a few more tips to read during your next rest stop:

You don't have to cut your hair into any style that starts with *duck* to be a lesbian or you'll forever refer to this period as "the time of the unfortunate haircut".

It's okay that you didn't like S. He's hot, and he certainly liked you. But it's a hopeless road to make yourself like anyone. Trust yourself.

Your heart belongs to her, no matter how many people push you to like a guy.

When you fall in love, the only one you'll want is her, even if she's 3,000 miles away.

Trust your intuition. It's your greatest gift. It's not the devil, honey. Call it your *bullshit detector*. And yes, you'll know within minutes on a first date. You'll just know.

Women can be players. Don't take it personally — and you're not one at heart.

Sometimes a weekend of sex is simply that. Don't make it into a two year relationship.

Don't believe it when "they" say that you have to work hard to enjoy life. It's a lie. Be a beautiful dreamer. *Live your bliss* isn't merely a nice idea but the irony is that you'll swim again a tide of naysayers if you *actually do*.

You'll be able to live on your own in NYC. Don't have roommates.

It's okay if you don't go out on Friday nights. You're not a loser, just built differently. Give yourself quiet and time to recharge in Nature. It's essential.

You don't like beer because you have a wheat allergy. Too much wine gives you migraines. You're perfectly healthy. Ease your mind as often as possible.

You're not possessed if you want a woman. You're not going to hell. Make peace with this in your own time. Come out only when it feels safe.

Those dreams are telling you that you're psychic. Someday it will be your work. Crazy, right? You're a healer but can't see it now because of all that rage. It's okay. I love who you are and I'm with you. Always.

DREAMIN'

I've been dreaming of cities. Silvery, shimmery cities that rise from the ocean.

San Francisco, to be exact.

I'm usually off in the distance or up on a hill in total darkness — but the lights of the city draw me in. They make me glad.

I have one purpose in mind: get there.

Much of "real life" is a fascinating puzzle to me — in contrast to my vibrant, active dreamworld. I visit places around the planet, have amazing conversations with people who are familiar and often feel confused upon waking. I have to remind myself of who and where I am.

Vermont showed up for years in my dreams when I thought I'd never leave New York City. They were lovely omens of a time to come that would teach me about community, family and love. Of course, I resisted and tried to shape them in a direction that would work. A part-time gig. Nope. Vermont wanted all of me.

The dream that sealed the deal? I sat crosslegged on the right wing of a 747 as we began our descent in the dark. The borders of Vermont were lit up like a runway in orange lights. I held a cup of coffee and said, "Hm. I wonder how I'm going to get back into the plane?" Then I shrugged and kept sipping my coffee.

My dreams offer amazing richness to my already beautiful life.

A few weeks later, I moved to a little town of which I knew nothing . . . and no one. Total population? 2,000 souls. Seven years on, I'm still here. The local Tarot reader.

Dreams are like water. As soon as you think you've got a handle on them, they shift.   They are portents. Maps. Hope builders. They say one thing: imagine.

Imagine: life without that nagging injury. Imagine life with a happy heart. Imagine goodness without strings. Imagine releasing the hate and anger you've carried for decades.

Dreams offer you that opportunity.

This is why it's wise to pay attention to the time right before sleep or waking. The body loosens her grip on "reality" and visions are more welcome. Answers easily come in symbols, colors or fragments of conversation. These gently odd signs can be the blazing clarity we've sought through therapists, psychics and the lot while upright.

San Fran? Maybe she's on my mind because of the changing times in California. Maybe I'll move back to a city.

It's okay that I don't know.

My visions don't require immediate change.

They simply say: imagine the possibilities.

I AM YOURS AND YOU ARE MINE

I am yours and you are mine.

You are mine and I am yours.

This is so, no matter how many you love. Marry. Care for.

No matter the years.

No matter how our bodies learn courage.

Our souls share ancient ground. Rooted and eternal.

I may never see you again in this lifetime.

I've made peace with my dead.

We are as connected as two aspen high in the Rockies.

Someday again, we'll meet.

Merge.

This I know.

There is a place for resolution.

A season of recognition.

We need to live, love.

Discover how big our soft hearts are.

But I am yours, and you are mine.

A simple fact that slumbers beneath my ribcage.

This you know.

I am the thought just beyond your left shoulder.

I am the remembrance of a time of grace when love came rushing in.

Love in, over and beyond us.

Love carried us in her torrent.

Cradled us in the ghetto.

Winged us to the far corners.

That same love in and around us even now.

The love who laughs at time.

Who says, *I am the essence of immortality. I will never die.*

I am yours and you are mine.

EVERYTHING IS DANCING

Floating.

Water hisses as it hits, baby liquid sluicing the larger body. Kids scream from the diving dock, "More rain! More rain!" and the thumping of their feet launches an underwater percussion. Thump, thump, thump.

You are here and hear but you are not present. You lay in the space between water and air. Colors undulate in a dance of their own vibration. You extend both arms but there is no solidity. Only water.

You are water.

Ears fill. Eyes close. Open, and rain patters straight into sockets. Tears rise. Kids scream. Thump, thump, thump. You float. Your heart is calm.

Stretching fingers as far as they go, you send slow swirls of sonic love — offering what you can.

To the water. To them. To her.

Green mountains circle and sway in approval.

Everything is dancing.

UNIVERSE: WORDS WITHOUT END

In the end, the names don't matter.

Call yourself a truck driver, Tarot reader or the Queen of Sheba.

It doesn't matter.

Want to heal the world?

Find your voice.

Then use it.

Tell your story.

COPYRIGHT PAGE

Copyright © 2013 Raven Mardirosian

GRATITUDE AND LOVE

Karen, thank you for the countless hours you spent throwing cards with me at that little table in the Moon Dog. You changed this Tarot reader's life.

To Bebe and Bernie. When I think of powerful women, I think of you both. Thank you.

To all of my teachers, guides and mysterious angels: I am forever grateful.

To my chosen familia worldwide: love, love, love. And more love.

Lakshmi, Durga, Tara, Venus, Ganesha -- thank you for helping me see the Goddess.

Deep love to all of my clients over the years. Your stories continually inspire me. Thank you for supporting and believing in my work.

And thank you, dear readers. Hope you enjoyed the ride.

ABOUT RAVEN

Raven Mardirosian is the author of 13 books, most notably *The Reluctant Tarot Reader: Adventures in the Gypsy Trade*. Her essay, "Christian LGBT Kids: You're Part of the Plan" is included in the New York Times bestselling anthology by Dan Savage and Terry Miller, *It Gets Better: Coming Out, Overcoming Bullying and Creating a Life Worth Living*.

Her other transformational books include: *Home: Thoughts On Belonging; Just Another Crazy Cat Lady Story; 365 Ways To Keep It Real, Heal Yourself and Be Free; Spirit, Flow: A Photographic Prayer; The Words Remain; We Dream Anew; Chrysalis: Poems of Release* and *Esprit, Vole: Prière photographique*. She has published 4 works of fiction under a nom de plume and created a relaxation DVD with Dr. William Kelley, *An Hour of Peace: Words, Music and Images for Relaxation*.

Raven developed and hosted the popular podcast, "Tarot Talk". She holds an M.A. in English with additional graduate studies at Bread Loaf School of English. Raven was a high-school English teacher for many years. She is now a sought-out spiritual teacher and intuitive guide who has helped thousands of clients for 14 years. Known for her humor, sensitivity and insight, Raven continues to offer her gifts to the world.

Follow her adventures at shivayawellness.com.

Made in the USA
Monee, IL
18 May 2020